**GRATITUDE**

This book was made possible with a fund from OSISA (Open Society Initiative for Africa).Thank you for your generous fund which went a long way towards writing, editing, and final publishing.  Special mention goes to Lucinda Van den Heever and Siphosami Malunga for understanding this project and for the encouragement. I will always be grateful!

My gratitude to ZIMRIGHTS (Zimbabwe Human Rights Association) for facilitating the project.

The National Archives of Zimbabwe played an all –embracing role as an invaluable store house of historical material. Thank you.

**DEDICATION**

This book is dedicated to my mother Canaan (MaDube) Jenje the first woman politician/activist/community leader I knew and to all the women politicians who have travelled our political space. It is on your shoulders that we stand, we women of today as we try to navigate today's political space.

*Gertrude Chibhagu, Joyce Jenje Makwenda and Margaret Zinyemba (2011)*

# THE HISTORY OF
# WOMEN POLITICIANS OF ZIMBABWE

**Joyce Jenje Makwenda**

# The History of Women Politicians of Zimbabwe
By Joyce Jenje Makwenda

Joyce Jenje-Makwenda
Collection Archives

Published by Joyce Jenje Makwenda
© Joyce Jenje Makwenda (2023) (2020,2013,2009 2002, 1998,1995)
Joyce Jenje Makwenda Collection Archives (JJMCA)
HARARE, Zimbabwe
Tel: +263 -242 -306623/306336
Cell:+263-773 468 378/775 22 0026
Email: joycejenje@gmail.com / email: jjmcaarchives@gmail.com
Website: https//wwwfacebook.com/joycejenjearchives

A record of this book is available at the National Archives of Zimbabwe

Besides the book, this project History of Women Politicians of
Zimbabwe also includes a Feature Film Documentary and Workshops.

ISBN 978-1-77924-769-8

*Joyce Jenje Makwenda and Tabitha Khumalo (2011)*

# Publication credits

| | |
|---|---|
| Researcher/Author: | **Joyce Jenje Makwenda** |
| Assistant Coordinator/ Transcriber: | **Yolanda Birivadi** |
| Short stories Editor (Some of): | **Sarudzayi Chifamba Barnes** |
| Cover Design: | **Jeffrey Milanzi** |
| Most of the photos: | **Fidelis Zvomuya** |
| Layout: | **Yolanda Birivadi** |
| Design and Layout: | **Jeffrey Milanzi** |
| Printed by: | **Sable Press** |

# TABLE OF CONTENTS

# MEDLEY

We addressed thousands of women ……..When I addressed people in Highfields I did not address 300 or 3,000, I addressed more than 30, 000, 00 and from there people would go and riot. That is why they took me to Gonakudzingwa. **(Ruth Chinamano - 1995)**

I wanted to breakdown the Land Apportionment Act, which I thought was an unnecessary act. One thing we did though in Garfield's parliament was when Herbert Chitepo returned from England as a fully-fledged lawyer under the Land Apportionment Act, he could not have offices in town. We actually passed a law allowing him to have an office in town. **(Muriel Rosin - 1995)**

It's good for women to venture into politics because politics decides the way a country should go, so women must be a part of that decision-making process but unfortunately sometimes personal egos hamper this set-up. We sometimes become too greedy, sometimes we want to challenge each other over nothing. I believe we should focus with the agenda of promoting women in the manner that it should be, the manner is don't challenge a woman who is already in a position, get the positions that the men are holding so that you become more in the set-up. What is the point of having 10 women out of 160 men? It does not work. Then you go there and you fight for those 10 posts.

While the women's wing is good for development, it should not keep them away from the male domain especially during elections. You are there, you are fixed up, at a corner somewhere doing your own thing as women, that's why we are still challenging each other so much and because of that we are not getting there. **(Eunice Sandi Moyo - 2011)**

We would get a group of five people; one Black, two Whites and a Coloured or two Indians and Blacks; go into a hotel to order tea or drinks. We were always being thrown out **(Eileen Haddon - 1992)**

I have been involved with women's work for the past decade and I have always wanted to play a role in the political arena of the country. I remember during my young days, when I was still a young girl, dating back in the 60's in Bulawayo I actually contested for a seat to be a Board Member. During those days Africans were actually contesting as Board Members but white people were Councilors. So I won a sit in Bulawayo. **(Betty Mtero – 2002)**

My direction into education became something that made me realise the importance for others. As you know the large masses didn't have the same opportunities. **(Diana Mitchell -1998)**

What made me join politics is that I grew up seeing a lot of inequalities. I worked very hard as a nurse, and it took me a lot of time to be promoted. I started in 1964 working at the Fort Victoria Hospital and I was the only black state registered nurse. So my promotion took longer because I got married. They said I was married so they could not place me where they wanted. Young nurses would come from the UK which were called Sunshine nurses and they would be promoted but I am the one who was doing the work for them. That showed me that I need to fight for my rights and that is what made me to be political conscious. That is why I was once president of the Nurses Association, then President for Women in Business. It is because I was fighting for the rights of nurses and also fighting for the rights of women in business. **(Maina Mandava – 2011)**

Right when I was fifteen years is when I joined the liberation struggle. In fact one thing I am happy about is when I joined the liberation struggle ......In fact I was not recruited by anyone. I took an initiative on my own that is why you find that I am so independent. I don't belong to individuals. Nobody can tell me to say 'It's me who recruited you from your school' In fact what I can say is that my family was highly political. I must have inherited it from my family. **(Margaret Dongo- 2002)**

 When we were preaching teaching other women about politics we were holding Bibles as if we were conducting church business and yet we were engaged in politics. So we were able to teach other women and they became interested in politics. **(Agnes Dete 2011)**

Let's keep the bird we have in hand, those are the members who are already there and now let's try to have more birds in hand so that we, at the end of the day we have 105 women in Parliament and men will be 105. It's not an easy thing to sell because already a lot of men are negotiating - Nyamupinga this issue of yours of 50/50 you want to take us out of Parliament? You know that 70 men must move out of Parliament to open space for the women! **(Beater Nyamupinga - 2011)**

But the question is who is voting for those men. We constitute 52% of the population. Go to those meetings you will find that women will be in the majority but what happens? Eeh, I would like to nominate that man putting on a red shirt sitting over there. There is a woman sitting next to her and she knows that woman by name. It's Thokozani Khupe, but she will then say aah, I am nominating that man in a red shirt over there. She doesn't even know the name of the man. **(Thokozani Khupe – 2011)**

Let me say that in parliament a woman should be brave. If I am saying a brave woman I mean a woman who does not see herself as a woman. A woman who looks at herself as a human being. There is no difference between men and women. As I have mentioned, men want to think they know everything. I remember when I was in parliament  at times when a  woman would stand up wanting to contribute you would hear men saying Bejing, Beijing and one would wonder where this Beijing is coming  from, and yet we did not learn of women's rights in Beijing. Women's rights is something that we have been talking about here at home. Men go to many conferences but it does not mean that they will be addressed by those conferences **(Angeline Masuku – 2002)**

The thing is we would like to encourage men in our homes to be the ones who support us than for us to be advocating for ourselves. Our husbands should feel proud that our wives are in high positions. Is it not good to be the husband of the president, or be the husband of a minister? If men did not see it the way I see it, but if they listen to the way I am explaining it, they may see it in a positive way. To be known as the husband of a Councillor  - it is a very good thing because you will have the first hand information regarding the development of your area because your wife will be having something to do with it and it's actually something that we should be proud of, than to say women should not be in politics. Instead, our husbands should be the ones encouraging us to be in politics and to participate in politics even if we do not agree, but that is the truth. Where you walk, its politics where you drink water, its politics **(Patricia Ndlovu - 2011)**

# INTRODUCTION

The history of women politicians dates back to time immemorial. During the pre-colonial days women's political position in the society was very strong. It was strong in the sense that women participated actively in all spheres of the society in Zimbabwe and the rest of Africa, there were women who as chiefs and queens were very respected by their society. Ambuya Nehanda (Charwe Nyakasikana) and Queen Lozikeyi are some of the women who held the highest political/leadership positions in Zimbabwe during the 1890's.

Besides holding the highest political positions in the society women had control of the economy of their communities; they had their own fields and their harvesting. They would store their food in their own granary. They built their own homes from foundation to the roof. Women were also educators in the sense that besides nurturing children and being the primary educator, they were also story tellers and would pass the history of the family to the new generation. In this context women were custodians of the values of the society and this gave them a much stronger voice in the society.

**Ambuya nehanda**        **Queen Lozikeyi**

**Women building a home**

**Woman telling stories to children**

All the activities that women were engaged in, during the pre-colonial era are closely intertwined with politics, and women can practically handle them all well. Politics is about economic power, accessing information and disseminating it, the right to protest, consciousness of cultural identity - women played a pivotal role in

**Ambuya Nehanda Maternity Hospital**

NEHANDA
NYAKASIKANA

# QUEEN LOZIKEYI

Queen Lozikeyi, King Lobengula's senior wife, took over the reigns of the Ndebele nation in 1894 when the nation was in turmoil after King Lobengula's disappearence. Lozikeyi is argued to be one of the best political strategists in the history of Zimbabwe's military history, making sure that the military was well equipped during the 1896 rebellion. She is argued to have led a better, well organized rebellion of 1896 than the 1893 rebellion (Marieke, Nyathi). Like Nehanda, she too inspired the ZIPRA's war during the 1970's war. According to Jeremy Brickhill (ZIPRA Force), the ZIPRA fighters buried two bullets, one FN and one AK, at the queen's grave. The FN bullet represented the Rhodesian forces, while the AK bullet represented the guerrillas. The ZIPRA soldiers did this to inform Queen Lozikeyi's spirit that the country was at war and to ask her for strength.

Pathisa Nyathi explains how the ZIPRA forces buried two bullets at Queen Lozikeyi's grave and what kind of a person Lozikeyi was. Pathisa Nyathi who has done an extensive study on Lozikeyi and the African culture explains how and why the ZIPRA Forces had to go to Queen Lozikeyi's grave to tell her that the country was at war and to ask for her guidance.

*When Africans went to war they always sought spiritual power and during the armed struggle in the 70's, Zipra was doing the same with regards to the grave of the Queen Lozikeyi. They took two bullets, one FN and the other AK that our liberation movements both ZANLA and ZIPRA were using.*

*They deposited the two as a way of informing the queen who was associated with war and playing a critical role during the 1896 war and at the same time requesting for success in that war and indeed that war was won and we went for elections in 1980.*

*Father Zimbabwe – Joshua Nkomo also visited the grave of Queen Lozikeyi before embarking on the struggle.*

*It was only proper that she be approached when the war started, the armed struggle. Joshua Nkomo had himself gone to Dududula. I think in 1954 there about in the company of Grey Mabhalale Bangu and William Chivago to request for Blessings and to announce that there were going to embark on a struggle. Nationalist at that stage, they went to Lozikeyi.*

Lozikeyi is argued to have been one of the richest people in the history of Zimbabwe. She maintained a balance between political power and economic power.

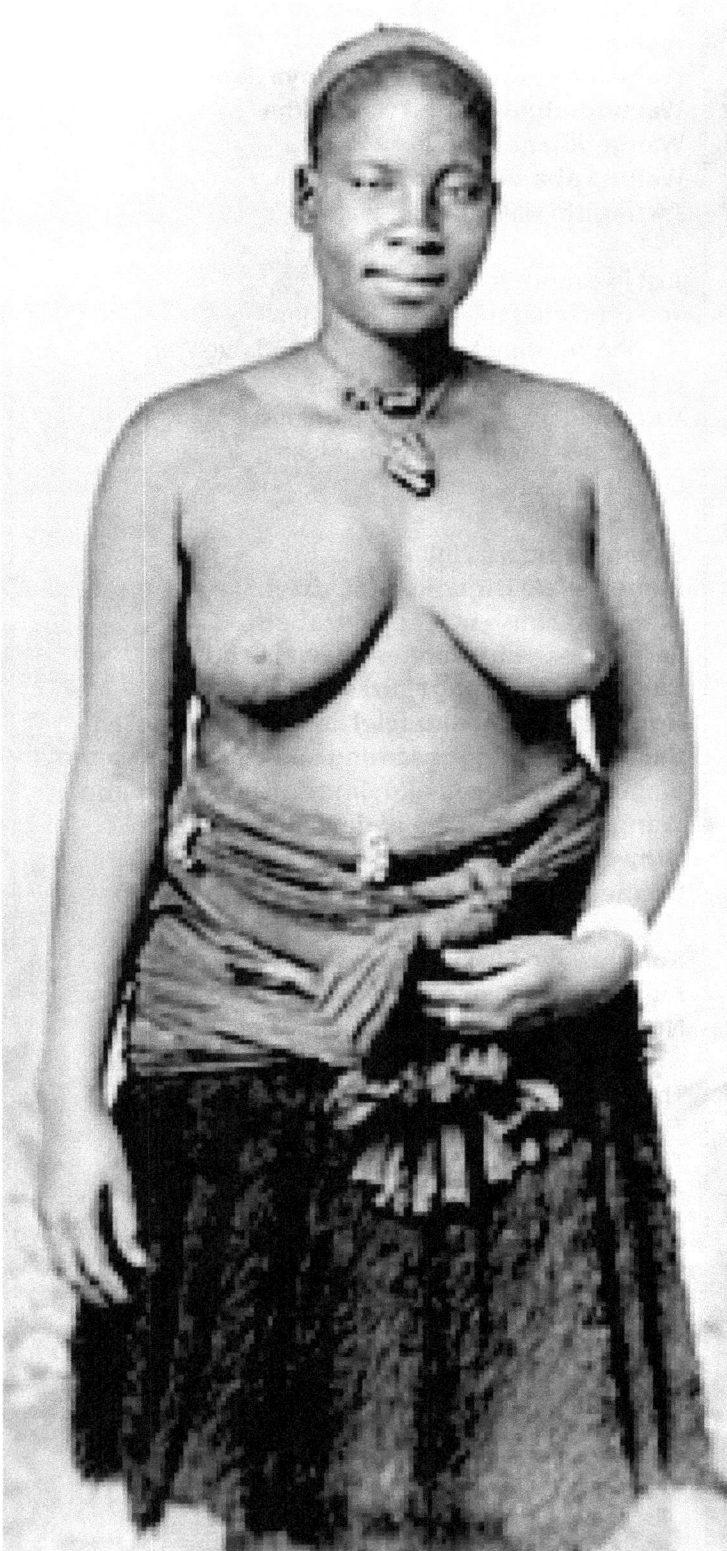

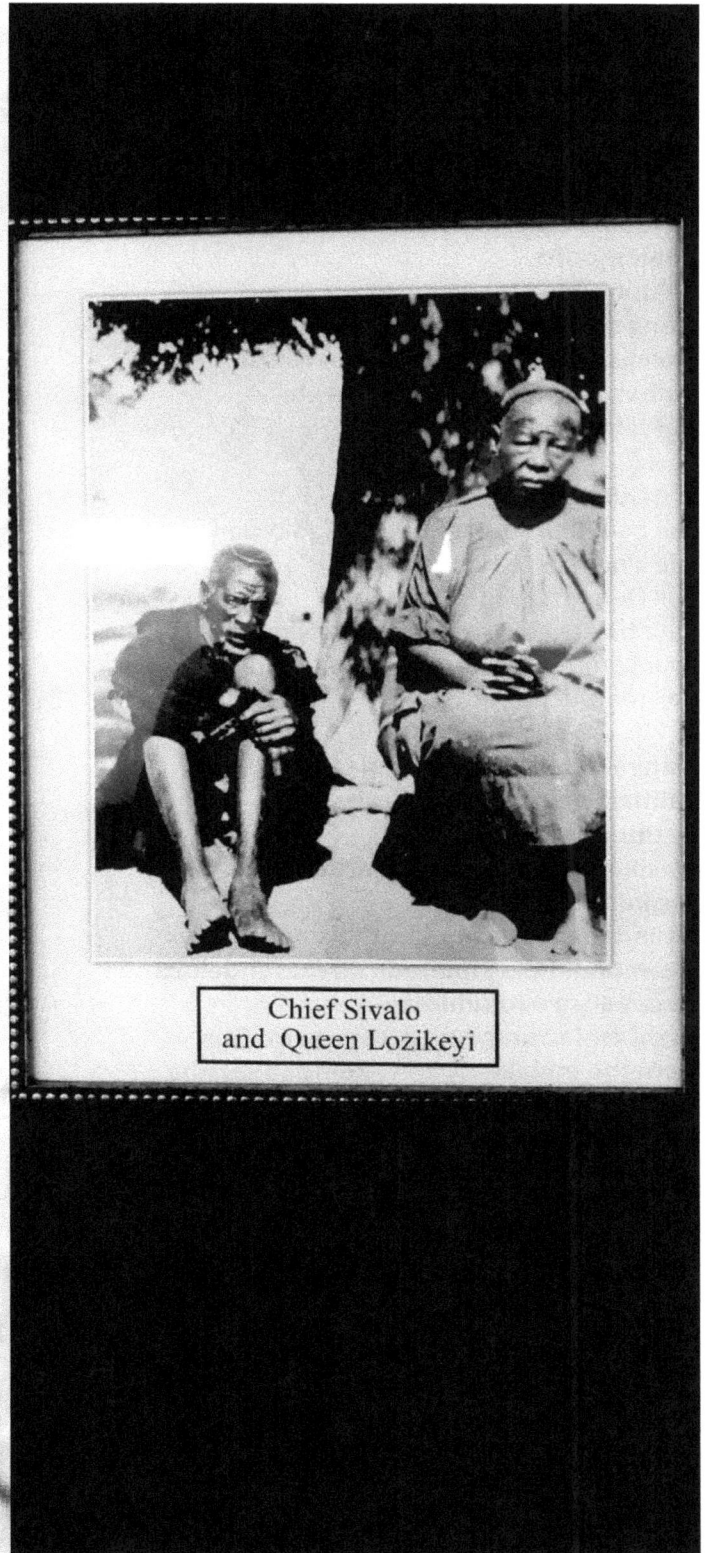

Chief Sivalo
and Queen Lozikeyi

# Queen Lozikeyi

*POEM BY STHANDAZILE DUBE*

**Ndlovukazi Lozikeyi**
**MaDlodlo omuhle**
**Qhube elingela qhwala**
**Iqhwala kulidolo lokuguqa nje qha**
**Mbanjwa zimagoda**
**Ziziquma zizithikelezela**
**Khalompofu**
**Khalomuhle**
**Wena onhliziyonhle**
**oncelisa bonke abantwana beNkosi**
**Osihawu Siwela umfula ugcwele**
**Ngiyakuvuma Ndlovukazi**

The Queen
The beautiful Lozikeyi of the Dlodlo clan
The kind hearted Queen
Hail Queen Lozikheyi
Who breastfeeds all the king's children
Your compassion knows no boundaries
Hail the Queen

**Wanyamalala uLobhengula wabawaba**
**Bakhala abafo labafokazana**
**Bezibona ubuntandane**
**Wasikhokhela isizwe samaNdebele**
**Saqiniseka esithi**
**Intandane enhle ngekhothwa ngunina**
**Wawakhokhela amadoda alamasendekazi**
**Baze bafisa ukukuhlola**
**Bethi mhlawumbe ulengisile kanti Cha**
**Uphethe inhlakanipho yakoMpangazitha**
**Ukhandakazi libuchopho bukhaliphile**
**Ngiyakuvuma Ndlovukazi**

King Lobhengula disappeared
The nation was in mourning
They thought they were orphans
Then along you came Queen Lozikeyi
You led the Ndebele nation
You led big and powerful men
They even thought you are a man disguised as a woman
But alias
You were endowed with the Dlodlo wisdom
Oh hail Queen

**Njengesikhukhukazi sivikela amatsiyane aso**
**Wasifukamela isizwe samaNdebele**
**Yimpumputhe yakuphi**
**Engaphatha eyehloka elibomvu ingalithinti elakho igama**
**Wamelana labondlebe zikhanya ilanga**
**Wavumbulula izikhali wakhokha**
**Wangqikilana labo**
**Wajuqa abajuqekayo**
**Awungithi bayethe qhawekazi**

Just like mother hen
You protected the Ndebele nation
No one will dare talk of the The Red Axe War
without mentioning your name
You stood up against the colonialist
Faced them head on without fear
Oh hail Queen

**Bayambabaza uZinkabi**
**Bamethulela isigqoko umkabayi**
**Bamphakamise uQueen Elizabeth**
**Lathi asiwuvali umlomo ngaweLozikheyi**
**Bakubiza isigebengakazi sakoMthwakazi**
**Ngoba ungafuni ukudelelwa ngumtakamesisi**
**Bakufakela imigoqo lemingcele endaweni yakho**
**Wakutshaya indiva okuyimithetshwana kwabo**
**Wangena waphutsha endaweni zabo**
**Uthwele imvubu**
**Ubanemba bebhense**
**Utshaya Indoda ihlengezele inyembeze**
**KoBulawayo kukomfazi utshaya Indoda nje**
**Kungenxa yezenzo zakhomaDlodlo**
**Ngithi tshaya Ndlovukazi tshaya**

They praise Zinkabi
They honor Mkabayi
They worship Queen Elizabeth
We hail you Queen Lozikeyi
They refer you as the 'gangster' of Mthwakazi (Bulawayo)
Because you did not want to be taken for granted
The colonialists erected boundaries for you in your home
You ignored the boundaries
And sjamboked them
They cried like babies

**Uyingwenyamakazi eyinkuzikazi
iqhawekazi elisibindikazi
Inkosikazi eyindlovukazi
Umfazikazi oyintandokazi
uqhumakazi ongumlamulankuzi**

You are a lioness
A she bull
A brave heroine
A Queen
A true woman
You are a peacemaker

**Bayethe mabanga
Bayethe msisiza omawakawaka
Bayethe ntingi kabangele
Sokhungwayo ngokukhungwa ngamadoda abesuthu
Somakhongo
Mqamlankungu kwazulu kwavela ilanga
Mbodlagazi ngomlomo
Wabhodla igazi kwachitheka amadoda
Thumbu wendlunkulu
Owahluba imfe zimbili kwaphuma ikhasi lilinye
Phiqilika okwetshongololo linengiwe
Haqo babayo
Sankunya sikamdladlama
Mabandla
Mawanga**

Hail Queen
Hail Queen
**- Poem by Standazile Dube**

One cannot therefore doubt that Mbuya Nehanda and Queen Lozikeyi are the foremothers of Zimbabwe's liberation.

Zimbabwe managed to produce such powerful women because the role of a woman in the society was powerful during the pre-colonial era.

*Queen Lozikeyi (sitting in the middle) with the other royal wives of King Lobengula*

# COLONIAL ERA 1950'S – 1960'S

# COLONIAL ERA
## 1950'S – 1960'S

The introduction of the colonialist systems saw the position of the African woman being weakened in the society.

African women disappeared from almost all the structures that controlled the country and they became invisible in the history of the country.

White women were not significant either, partially because they were still very few of them in the colony. When white women became more visible in later years they were still regarded as second class citizens. This is how Doris Lessing interpreted the role of white women in colonial society: *"The woman was not considered to be an equal to man. The White Rhodesian woman had to be pretty, a social asset to her man…. Their only power, indeed, lay in their control of household servants. Some women did enter the labour force but, for most part, their jobs - as secretaries, for example – merely extended their roles as the providers of services to men. Those who joined a profession were seen as odd."*

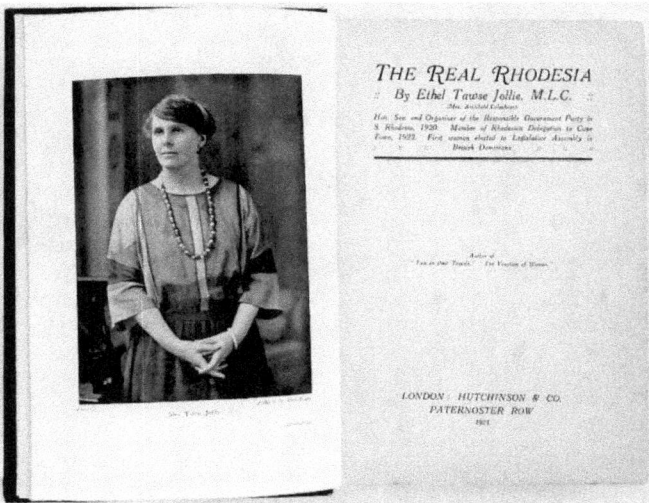

*Tawse Jolly*

*Tawse Jolly in the 1923 government*

THE REAL RHODESIA
By Ethel Tawse Jollie, M.L.C.

LONDON : HUTCHINSON & CO.
PATERNOSTER ROW

**Ethel Tawse Jolly (First women MP in Southern Rhodesia)**

White women did not enjoy the public space as their male counterparts and under this environment women could not even dream of being politicians. However, there were a few outstanding women like Muriel Rosin (1953), who made an impact across the racial divide and before her there was Tawse Jolly who was elected the first woman MP in Southern Rhodesia (1923). In (1929) there was Miss KM Davidson who was later Mrs. Gale.

*KM Davidson*

*KM Davidson in the 1929 governement*

*Muriel Rosin*

*Muriel Rosin in the federal governement*

## Women and Politics of the 1950's -1960's

It was not until the 1950s and the 1960s that black women began participating in modern day politics. Women got fed up with the political situation and decided to take back their place in the society as decision-makers. They realised that they could not continue to stand on the sidelines as they had to be involved in the running of their affairs which were controlled by politics.

One of the ways to get through to the oppressive government was to organize protest marches. Some of the women who were involved in early politics (1950's, 60's) were, Ruth Chinamano, Sally Mugabe, Victoria Chitepo, Thenjiwe Lesabe, Sunny Ntombiyelanga Takawira, Julia Zvobgo, Mai Murape, Mai Nyamurova and Jane Ngwenya.

### Ruth Chinamano (1925 – 2005)

***Ruth Chinamano***

Ruth Chinamano was the first woman political detainee at Gonakudzingwa, after leading a women's protest against colonial injustices against women by the government of the 50's. The authorities were angered by the mob of women who had come to challenge them. Ruth Chinamano remembered how tense the situation was. *They would have loved to shoot us but they didn't, we were bitten by the dogs. Later on we addressed a meeting in Highfield of more than 30 000 and after that people went rioting. That is why they sent me to Gonakudzingwa (detention).* Said Ruth Chinamano in an interview in 1994. Ruth participated in national politics during the federation of Rhodesia and Nyasaland, the UDI and post-colonial Zimbabwe. She put her country first before her children. In April 1964, Chinamano was detained at Gonakudzingwa with her husband, Josiah Chinamano, the late Vice President Joseph Msika and Father Zimbabwe Joshua Nkomo. They were the first four inmates at the prison and she being the only woman. She and her husband were transferred to Hwahwa Prison where they remained until 1970. When they were released they were confined to an 8km radius restriction but were arrested again only to be released in 1974. Ruth Chinamano was reunited with her children after 10 years in 1975.

Ruth Chinamano, husband and children

She held different posts in Zapu, and when Zimbabwe attained its independence in 1980, she held various posts in Zapu and Zanu PF and the government. She was one of the 8.6% of women elected to parliament on a PF ZAPU ticket from 1980-1985, she later became a member of the ZANU PF Central Committee after the ZAPU and ZANU Unity Accord in 1987. She also continued to encourage women to take their place in the political arena and supported the electing of Joice Mujuru as Vice President of the party and of the country.

**Ruth Chinamano takes us through her political journey and when she came to Zimbabwe then Rhodesia.**

*I came to Rhodesia in 1950. When I got here I realised what my husband had told me that there was worse colour bar in Rhodesia than in South Africa. At least in South Africa you will see Europeans only or non-Europeans signs and here you go to the park, this park which is in front of our parliament. We used to sit anywhere and we would see the police chasing you and yet there was nothing written. It was a snakish one and yet in South Africa you knew where to go and you found the same comfortable seats like those of the white people. So I came here with that in mind because even before I came here I took part in politics myself when I was a small child. My father was a politician and he used to address thousands not to carry passes and he used to be arrested every day and my own father suffered. He was called a jailbird because of teaching people politics from Queenstown, East London and Cape Town.*

Ruth Chinamano lived in Mbare when she came to Zimbabwe then Rhodesia. Later on she and her husband Josiah Chinamano got teaching jobs at Marshal Hartley School.

*So I saw it all, from Mbare I went to Marshall Hartley to teach, from Marshall Hartley I went to Waddilove to teach and when I was in Waddilove we were sent to Britain both my husband and I, and I took Community Development there. I used to go to Hyde Park on Sundays and listen to different kinds of politicians from all over the world speak freely there. That was my food. Even when I was taking Community Development. I specialised on public speaking and when I got home here in 1957, I went back to my teaching place in Waddilove but on Fridays I used to go to Highfields now were there was a branch, and then I used to meet the women there and join them. Go back to teach and then Friday I would go there and this meeting was held behind Mwayera (Mwayera shop).*

It was not easy for civil servants - a teacher or nurse then to engage in politics but Ruth Chinamano being a teacher despised that law and she became involved in politics.

So those women who were educated as teachers or nurses feared politics because those days there was a law – white law that if you are a teacher you cannot join politics. That was also a kind of oppression of the blacks by whites, but mina (me) I broke that. I broke that. I used to come here in Higfields and attend political meetings, join demonstrations. One of the first demonstration I joined with the white women who were interested in the country, who fought with the Africans....

Joyce – Do you remember the women?
Ruth Chinamano – Mrs Margaret Moore, Claton Brook, Yates and all those women, there were interested and Ranger, Mr. and Mrs Ranger. Those white women, I was the only black women. Elina, yoo Elina this woman

Joyce – Mrs. Haddon
Ruth Chinamano – Yes Mrs Haddon. We staged the first black demonstration outside parliament those days, there was Whitehead who was called the Golden Moll. He was a Prime minister that time and we were demonstrating against the detention of Chikerema, Madzimbamuto, George Nyandoro and others in Gokwe.

**Ruth Chinamano, with other women talking to Eileen Haddon who had visited them in detention**

We were beaten by dogs. When I addressed meetings at Highfields, I didn't address 10 people or 300 or 3,000. I addressed more than 30,000 and from there people would go and riot. That's why they took me to Gonakudzingwa. We were taken to Gonakudzingwa on the 16th of April in 1964. We stayed at Gonakudzingwa for a year and we thought that we were going to be released after a year and after a year the

detention was extended. The detention was extended until 11 years. We were moved from restriction area to restriction area, in another part of the country and from prison to prison, not only in one prison. Next time to Khami prison. The first people to be detained to get such a detention were Mr. Nkomo, Mr. Msika, Mr. Chinamano and myself.

**Josiah Chinamano, Ruth Chinamano and Daniel Madzimbamuto at Gonakudzingwa**

The first to be detained at Gonakudzingwa. The boundary of Portuguese East Africa (Mozambique) and Zimbabwe near Villa Salaza where these policeman who guarded us lived. We were not allowed to cross the road to go to their police station because they thought we were going to be devoured by lions. Now Gonakudzingwa was that to know how to drive away misfits from the community.

The four of us. We didn't know what we were going to do? We thought we were going to be killed. But to our happiness and something which gave us strength a man who was a worker in the train from Salisbury to Villa Salaza stoll at night and found us where we were and told us that we should not fear because when we were taken away all the women went on bicycles, cars, on foot, on trucks, in front of the prison to say that we want to go where Mrs Chinamano has gone. She has left her children we must also leave our children. They went there to be arrested. That was unique and it showed the solidarity of women, before the split. The women took action, the likes of Amai Nyamurova.

**Ruth Chinamano**

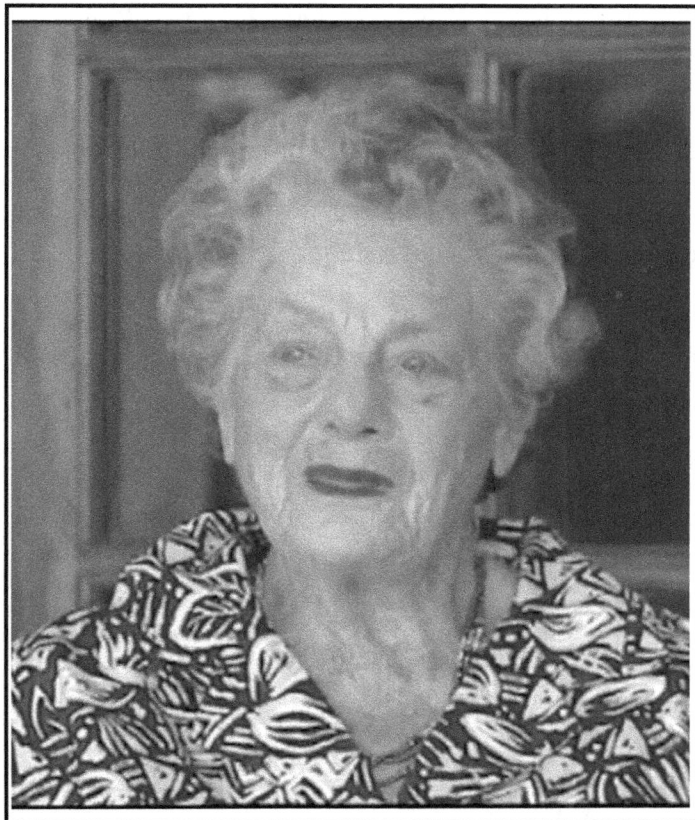

**Muriel Rosin**

## Muriel Rosin (1909 – 1999)

In the 1950's a rare white woman Muriel Rosin was the only woman MP in the Federal government during the Federation of Rhodesia and Nyasaland. Muriel was known as the 'only man' in the Federal government. Muriel found it easy to mix with men at all levels. It was easy for her to interact with men because she had gone to a CO ED school, which was very unusual in her days. In the interview that I had with her in the 90s, she said: *I think it was easier for me because I went to a conventional school, which was very unusual in my days so I got used to working with men. They respected me and they never ignored my ideas because I was just the same as them.*

Rosin made meaningful contributions and was not intimidated when it came to discussions in the parliament. During her time, Muriel made tremendous changes in the Territorial government which was responsible for African affairs. Housing was a territorial matter and when Muriel was in the Territorial government she was very instrumental in building Highfield Township. She also convinced the then government to turn the Beatrice

Cottages into a house ownership scheme which was an internal camp where mostly Italians and Germans had lived at the end of the war. Highfield and the Beatrice Cottages were the first to be under the home ownership scheme for black people, whereas people living in other townships like Mbare Township signed a lease for 99 years. Muriel also fought hard to try and have the Land Apportionment Act repealed, but unfortunately this was the weapon which the UDI used to win votes from the white populace. During UDI Muriel Rosin gave Smith a hard time. Smith had to send the secret service to her husband to try to refrain his wife (Muriel), as they were scared to face her.

Muriel Rosin gave us a brief of what it was like when she arrived in Zimbabwe then Rhodesia and what made her get interested in politics and her political career.

*I arrived here a new bride from London feeling very strange, thinking that I was coming in the middle of Africa, I found here very Victorian Provincial City amongst white people….. It was very Victorian.*

*I went to make them tea and poured in my cups and put some biscuits there and my mother in law and she said you don't do that if you want to give your stuff tea you put the tea there, the sugar and the milk and any biscuits you want to give them and they bring their own mugs. You don't give them your own cups. It was a terrible thing. I took a long time to get used to that, that there was a division between white and black. I could not understand.*

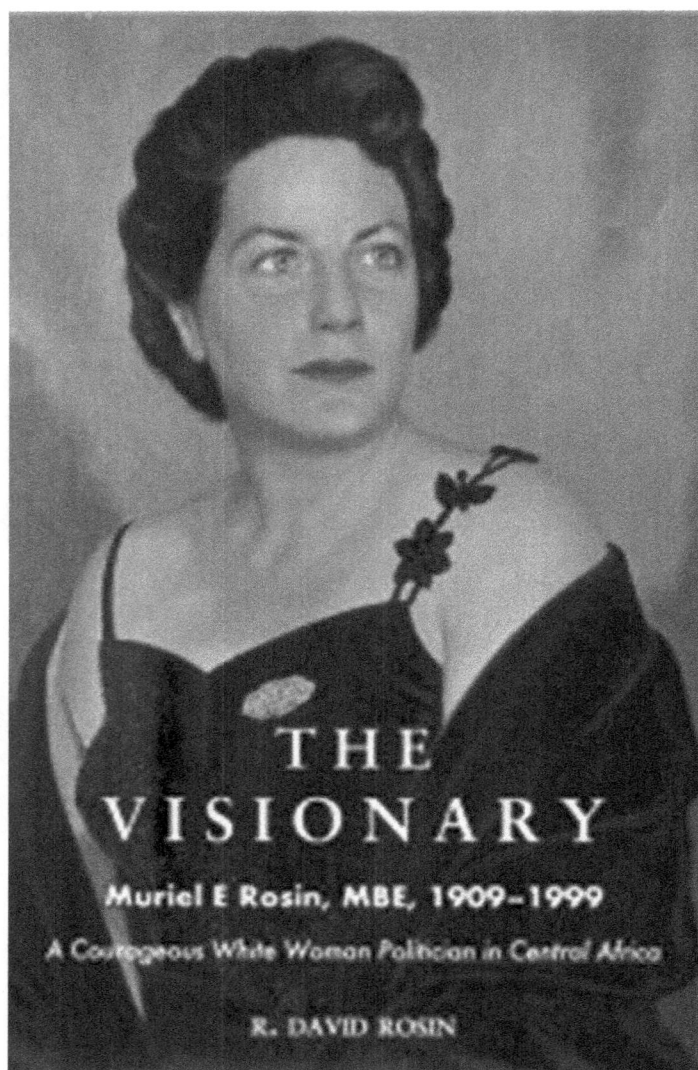

THE
VISIONARY

Muriel E Rosin, MBE, 1909-1999

A Courageous White Woman Politician in Central Africa

R. DAVID ROSIN

Muriel Rosin
August 1996

**Muriel Rosin**

*Well then I was with the Women's Institute then it became Southern Rhodesia Federation of Women's Institute. I went to see all these laws where we wanted change and nothing was happening you know. You could not get the government to move because (there wasn't money I suppose.) We wanted district nurses, we wanted level crossings, things of that kind, and were very citizen minded. Let me put it that way. Also my husband was asked if he could consider going into politics, he said don't ask me, ask*

*my wife. So he rather encouraged me to go into politics and that is what happened. Before that I had already joined the United Party as it was then and I later became chairman of the women's section and got more and more interested.*

*I was involved in United Federal Party when (Welensky, when Huggins, when Lord Malvin) was Prime Minister of the Federation and Garfield Todd was Prime Minister of Southern Rhodesia and I went into the Federation.*

*While the Federation of Rhodesia and Nyasaland was supposed to promote an inter-racial society. It turned out there were hard liner whites who were racists and did not respect the reason the Federation was mooted. However under Garfield Todd things started changing as he wanted to bring all the races together.*

*It started improving, it certainly improved under Garfield Todd who was I think an excellent Prime Minister. I served in his parliament and I was very sad when they kicked him out. It was a tragic occasion, really tragic, because he was the first man who was the Prime Minister both to black and white people and he was extremely good - liberating things, slowly but surely. Could not do it quickly otherwise you had very right wing whites fighting him all the time, anyway who would have objected. But it was very interesting. The first time I got into parliament under Garfield Todd I had Highfields in my constituency so I went around canvassing. I had always gone around and had quite a number of black friends and I had always been interested in the whole set up.*

Muriel fought hard to try and break the Land Apportionment Act but it was unfortunate that this is the weapon that Ian Smith and the UDI used.

*I wanted to breakdown the Land Apportionment Act, which I thought was an unnecessary act. One thing we did in Garfield's parliament was when Herbert Chitepo returned from England as a fully-fledged lawyer under the land apportionment act. He could not have offices in town. We actually passed a law allowing him to have an office in town because as a lawyer he would not have much of a practice of, if he had been in what was called African Areas.*

While Rosin applauded today's women for fighting hard to attain high posts in politics she wished there could be more women in parliament.

# WOMEN MARRIED TO THE STRUGGLE AND POLITICIANS IN THEIR OWN RIGHT

# Women married to the Struggle and Politicians in their own right

The 1950's – 1960's saw women being virtually married to the struggle. They married men who were political activists, most of whom were jailed and detained by the system. These women, later on, became politicians in their own right because of what was happening in their families and communities. They had no husbands most of the times and they had to raise children by themselves. The political situation in the country did not leave them any choice but to be politicians as well. Some of these women were; Joana Mafuyana, Sally Mugabe, Maud Muzenda, Maria Msika, Victoria Chitepo, Julia Zvobgo, Sunny Ntombiyelanga Takawira and Stella Madzimbamuto.

## JOANA NKOMO

**Joana Nkomo (Mama Mafuyana) – (1927 – 2003),** who married Joshua Nkomo (Father Zimbabwe) in 1949 was definitely married to the struggle. Her motherly love was national as it went beyond her immediate family to embrace the young cadres moving to and from

*Joana Mafuyana and family*

various training camps and refugee centres. At independence, up to her death, Mama Mafuyana worked for the unity of all Zimbabweans.

Joana Nkomo (Mama Mafuyana), was never to enjoy the company of her husband and accepting that she could lose or cede her husband to the struggle, made her a virtual widow. The couple was blessed with 4 children, with the husband's life fluctuating between long spells in detention and risky missions of the struggle, the burden of raising the family was hers. Single handedly, she fended for the family ensuring that the children secured decent upbringing and decent education.

Her strength and resourcefulness as a mother released her husband from family chores giving him time to focus on leading and prosecuting the struggle.

At independence, up to her death, Mama Mafuyana worked for the unity of all Zimbabweans; mostly for the welfare of underprivileged children through the Child Survival and Development Foundation. Her departure on the 3rd of June 2003 was a sad loss to the nation. She is buried at the national shrine.

*(Mama Mafuyana's article was taken from - ZBC Remembering Mama Mafuyana).*

## SALLY MUGABE

**Sally Mugabe (1931 – 1992)** was married to Robert Mugabe became the mother of the nation. At Independence she was popularly known as *'Amai'.* In 1962 she was active in mobilizing women to challenge the constitution which resulted in her being charged with sedition and sentenced to five years imprisonment, part of which was suspended.

*Sally and Robert Mugabe*

Sally Mugabe is one of the women who became active in politics in the 1960's and she became the founding mother of the new nation of Zimbabwe in 1980. She was popularly known as Amai (Mother) for the work she did for the country before and after independence.

She got married to Robert Mugabe in 1961, coming from an independent Ghana, Amai Sally was annoyed by open racial discrimination which was practiced in Rhodesia. Sally Mugabe demonstrated her political activism as early as 1962 when she was active in mobilizing women to challenge the constitution which resulted in her being charged with sedition and sentenced to five years imprisonment, part of which was suspended. In 1975 she joined her husband Robert Mugabe in Maputo, she found herself challenged to a new role of a mother figure to thousands of Zimbabwean refugees and revolutionaries. Her efforts in this role earned her the popular title *Amai* (Mother).

In the 1980's she founded the Zimbabwe Child Survival Movement. In 1981, she became the patron of Mutemwa Leprosy Centre in Mutoko and helped erase the social stigma associated with lepers. She also assumed patronage of many children's centres including disabled and orphaned children.

Amai Sally Mugabe also initiated projects aimed at rehabilitating prostitutes.

She launched the Zimbabwe Women's Cooperative in the UK in 1986 and supported *Akina Mama wa Africa,* a London based African women's organization focusing on development and women's issues in Africa and the United Kingdom.

Amai Sally Mugabe died of a kidney aliment on January 27 1992 and became the first heroine to be buried at the National Heroes Acre.

## MARIA MSIKA

*Maria and Joseph Msika*

**Maria Msika (1928 – 2017),** Maria Msika fended for the family when her husband, Joseph Msika, was jailed by the Rhodesian Regime. Mama Maria Msika was, herself, detained several times as a way of forcing her husband to come out of hiding.

She also participated in the demonstrations held in the 1960's together with the likes of Jane Ngwenya.

## MAUD MUZENDA

Simon Muzenda

Also known as "Mai Muzenda", **Mama Maud Muzenda (1928 – 2017),** worked as a nurse. She confronted the colonial government and administration, demanding improved working conditions for black professionals and equal treatment with their white counterparts. While the Black cadres were being arrested and detained by the racist Rhodesian regime, Mai Muzenda formed an underground movement to continue supporting the armed struggle. In addition, she treated injured freedom fighters and supplied them with medicine and even money.

## SUNNY TAKAWIRA

*Sunny Takawira and husband Leopold Takawira and children*

Mama **Sunny Ntombiyelanga Takawira** (Amai Takawira) – (1927– 2010), a nurse by proffession was married to Leopord Takawira in 1955, who served as the Vice President of ZANU after supporting the (NDP) and later ZAPU. Amai Takawira was never to enjoy her marriage as her husband was either in prison or abroad fundraising and mapping out strategies for the party. After the arrest of Cde Leopold Takawira in 1964, she smuggled letters and information in and out of prison at Hwahwa, Gonarezhou and Sikombela Detention Centers as well as Salisbury Central Prison. The couple had three children which she had to raise alone as her husband died mysteriously in prison in 1970.

Lindiwe Mimi Tsele intervied Amai Takawira in 1980; the death of her husband did not take away the resolve in Cde Sunny to work for the liberation of Zimbabwe. During her stint as a nursing sister at a clinic in Highfield near Mbizi Police Station, she contributed much to the liberation struggle through treating both civilians and those who were injured in the armed struggle. She was also involved in the demonstrations organized by the nationalists' wives whose spouses were languishing in detention. They often demonstrated against discrimination of the colonial regime with women such as Ruth Chinamano which resulted in them being detained at Harare Central Police Station, only to be released after paying fines. Her home was also attacked in 1979 resulting in her two children, Gertrude and Leopold Jnr being injured. (Lindiwe Mimi Tsele 1980)

In 1980, Amai Sunny Takawira was appointed Senator for Midlands. After the ceasefire in 1980, along with her two sons, came many freedom fighters to stay with her at the family house in Highfield. She continued well into independent Zimbabwe providing shelter to many war veterans. She believed in leading by example. For instance, in the early 1980s, together with Tsitsi Munyati and many other women, Amai Takwira participated in sponsored walks and charity events. In 1980 she walked from Melfort to Harare Post Office to raise funds for wounded war veterans at Melfort.

In1980, Amai Sunny Takawira was appointed Senator for Midlands.

Sunny Ntombiyelanga Takawira passed on, on the 3rd of January 2010 and she is one of the few women at the National Heroes Acre

## JULIA ZVOBGO

**Julia Zvobgo (1937 – 2004),** was also very active in politics in the 1960's up to the time of her death. She was part of a demonstration in the 1960's and she was pregnant, dogs were set on the women who had demonstrated and beaten but the police did not touch her because she was pregnant.

In 1964 her husband Eddison Zvobgo was arrested

*Julia Zvobgo*

*Eddison Zvobgo*

and sent to prison, which became difficult for her as she had to raise children alone. In 1968 she decided to leave the country, she went to the UK and then the United States. In 1977 she went to Mozambique during the height of the war, she came back in 1979 after the war and stood as an MP and she won, she was one of the few women MPs at independence. She is the third woman to be buried at the National Heroes Acre the National Shrine, not many women have been buried at the national shrine despite having fought the war just like their male counterparts.

## VICTORIA CHITEPO

*Victoria and Herbert Chitepo*

Between 1960 and 1961 **Victoria Chitepo (1928 – 2016)**, was leading various activities one of which was a women's sit in at Salisbury Magistrates' Court to promote the campaign for Black citizenship.

In 1975, Herbert Chitepo, her husband, was assassinated in Lusaka, Zambia. She remained in Tanzania until 1980 when Zimbabwe gained its independence.

## STELLA MADZIMBAMUTO

*Stella and Daniel Madzimbamuto*

In 1965 **Stella Madzimbamuto (1930 – 2020)** fought a landmark case, Madzimbamuto v Lardner-Burke, challenging the detention of her husband Daniel Madzimbamuto.

She maintained that the government of Rhodesia was an illegal state thus the imprisonment of her husband Daniel Madzimbamuto was unlawful. In the midst of all this she was raising her children alone and working as a nurse.

## EILEEN HADDON

*Mike Haddon*

Eileen Haddon and her husband were political activists in the 1950's and provided political detainees with legal aid. In an interview that I had with Eileen and Mike Haddon in 1992 they explained the situation then:

*The State of Emergency was declared on the 26th Februrary 1959 and 500 people were put in (detention), all of them black with the exception that was Guy Clutton - Brock and the Clutton Brock's were good friends of ours and when Guy was released after a month or so it was, he made the point that life was extraordinarily difficult for those detainees because they had no subsistence for the family and they were sitting and doing nothing in jail. No books to read and so on. So we set up this legal fund and welfare fund to provide, first of all, legal aid but also education for people in prisons who wanted to do degrees. Well that started off with people like George Nyandoro, James Chikerema.*

*But there were a lot of others from what is Malawi – David Rubhadheri. Then of course we continued visiting Dan Madzimbamuto for example he was one of the longest and we funded the case his wife Stella brought against the government for illegal imprisonment under the Law and Order Maintainance Act where she lost that one. But later after the UDI situation, no it was in 62, 63, there were a whole series of other arrests and people like*

*the Chinamanos', where pushed into Hwahwa, Willy Musarurwa was in Hwahwa, then in Gondakudzingwa, then Sikhombela.*

*I forget the name of the ZANU one, were Leopold Takawira. Was Sithole there? I can't remember but a lot of the people who are in the present government were detained either in Gonakudzingwa or in one of the other detention camps, and we did our best to supply them with funds – the wives and families. At that stage we were allowed in the prisons to educate. Ellenor Jefrey was one of the people who was good at that. But later they stopped our entry in the prisons altogether.*

The work Eileen Haddon and other progressive people had started, needed funding and some of the people like Colleen Collins in Britain supported them financially. Amnesty International supported the Interracial Association and according to Mike Haddon there were amongst the first group to be funded by Amnesty International. It was through the founder Peter Benenson.

# WOMEN'S CLUBS, WORKING WITH COMMUNITIES AND POLITICS

# Women's Clubs, Working with Communities and Politics

**W**omen's clubs played a very important role in uplifting women's lives in the 30's, 40's, 50s, 60's, and 70's and as a result some women became politically conscious through these organizations. Some of the women who were active in women's clubs were Betty Mtero, Helen Mangwende, Musodzi Ayema, Tsitsi Munyati, Mrs. Lesabe and Mai Mutsvairo. The work they did with the community made them aware of the political situation in the country.

*Mrs. Mabel Lesabe*

*Mrs. Victoria Mutsvairo*

**Betty Mtero (1932-2022)**

Another woman who got to understand politics through working with women's clubs and her community was **Betty Mtero**. Unfortunately because of how complicated politics has become she decided to take a step back. Mtero was always interested in council politics in order to help her community. While in Bulawayo in Njube, Betty Mtero helped in the building of the African Children's Helping Hand Crèche, which still stands to this day.

Because of her commitment to her community Betty Mtero was elected a Councilor for Njube, beating all the men who had contested. After independence she worked with the Ministry of Women's Affairs. Since then she was based in Harare and continued to be active in community issues, until her death in 2022.

**This is what Betty Mtero said in the interview I had with her in 2002:**

*I have been involved in women's work for the past decade and I have always wanted to play a role in the political arena of the country. I remember during my young days when I was still a young woman, dating back in the 60's in Bulawayo I actually contested to be a Board Member. During those days Africans were actually contesting as Board Members but white people were councilors. So I won a seat in Bulawayo and that time campaigning wasn't as bad as it is now. Actually what happened was one would let your aspirations known to people to the residents in the township and some of them would come and approach you to find out, to know if it was possible to represent them. That is why I am saying it wasn't as serious as today. So my campaign wasn't as serious as it is now, because, people had accepted already that I was going to be the candidate so it was actually a matter of encouraging people to vote in large numbers so I did won the election and I got a lot of support from both the women and men so that is how I really got involved in the Civic affairs of the community.*

*Today it's more complicated because I have tried, you know now and again to get involved myself in politics seriously now and especially that I work with women and part of it really when I announce that I am contesting it's a way to try and encourage other women to come and not be shy. To come up and be candidates in any election. First of all I was really surprised because you know I actually put forward my name to contest for the Mayors position in Harare.*

*I can't remember the year but I think it was the first time when the first mayor was Executive Mayor of Harare. I can't remember the year but I know that was the first that was going to be executive mayor in all the towns in the country. Some people thought I wasn't serious you know. They stipulated conditions of one who wanted to contest and as far as I was concerned I had the qualifications as required but to my surprise was that I got at times encouraging comments from men and women would say to me 'oh that is a big position I don't think you will be able to do it, one has to be first a councilor and they need somebody who would travel overseas to*

*solicit for funds to help the city.' You know they came up with all sorts of reasons and I knew I had travelled extensively throughout, not only in the country but outside the country. I have travelled for various reasons and so far as I was concerned I was once a councilor although it was like a Board Member (Black people then in the 1960's contested as Board Members and White people as councilors), so to me I qualified but the women did not sort of have confidence in me so I got more encouragement from men and not from women and this was really disappointing and then what turned up to be was that names had to be screened and in the end we heard that the politburo had actually selected the man who was going to be a mayor who was going to contest the seat in Harare so that's how I dropped in the contest.*

## MUSODZI AYEMA

**Musodzi Ayema** was a community leader in Mbare from the 1930s. She did this through various organisations, including women's clubs. Musodzi assisted the needy and illiterate in a variety of ways, be it physical education or home nursing. Some of her graduates later went on to work in hospitals. She founded women's clubs, and worked as a unifying force among foreigners and locals.

She was married to a Zambian. She hailed from the Hwata family (clan), origin of Mbuya Nehanda (Charwe) who was sister to her father. Despite the fact that her relatives perished during the Mashona uprising in Mazowe, Mai Musodzi was optimistic about life's brighter opportunities. She moulded a positive personality always yearning to make a meaningful contribution to society.

She pioneered Red Cross and Home Craft Clubs for Township women; all this unfolding at Mai Musodzi Hall, which was named after her. She was also honoured as MBE - Member of the British Empire.

## HELEN MANGWENDE

**Helen Mangwende** was a champion of rural clubs, she was married to Chief Mangwende. This helped women with better ways of managing their lives in every sphere. Helen gave birth to the Association of Women's Clubs (AWC), which is still in operation. Unfortunately she died a premature death but the work she started is still being carried on.

## TSITSI MUNYATI

*Tsitsi Munyati in black dress reading to children*

**Tsitsi Munyati** played an important role in the development of women through the Young Women's Club Association (YWCA) in Zimbabwe then Rhodesia which made a great impact on women in the 1970's. She was instrumental in building a crèche in Chitungwiza called the Early Learning Centre. Munyati was also a broadcaster and a television presenter in the 1970's and used the media to champion women's cause and also used it to challenge the Rhodesian racial segregation system. At independence she was appointed Deputy Minister of Education and Culture.

Her life was cut short in 1982 in a car accident.

Even today many women have been politically conscientised through working with their communities, because of responding to the needs of their communities some have ended up in parliament as the com-

munities feel they are the right people to represent them in parliament. Some have been in leadership roles outside parliament and this has also benefitted their communities.

Some of the women politicians who have worked with their communities are Angeline Masuku, Canaan Jenje, Sithembiso Nyoni, Elina Shirichena, Jenia Manyeruke, Gladys Mabhiza, Mavis Chidzonga, Margaret Dongo and more.

**Stembiso Nyoni**

**Elina Shirichena**

**Jenia Manyeruke**

**Gladys Mabhiza**

**Mavis Chidzonga**

**Margaret Dongo**

**Angeline Masuku** has been in politics since the 1960's (1963). She became secretary for Bulawayo District in North West Province.

When the political situation became untenable she left for Zambia to join ZIPRA the military wing of ZAPU. At independence she held different positions in ZAPU, ZANU PF and at national level.

When ZANU and ZAPU were negotiating the Unity Accord, Angeline was part of the high powered committee. The Unity Accord between ZANU PF and PF ZAPU was signed on December 22 in 1987.

Angeline Masuku was Member of Parliament for Luveve for 10 years, this was because of her involvement in community activities.

Angeline Masuku explains how she has worked with the community in her constituency of Luveve.

*The first thing that I did in the ten years I spent in par-*

**Angeline Masuku**

*liament which I also think will carry my name is that in Luveve Township there were only three secondary schools, even now (2002) they are still three but the secondary schools did not have "A" Levels.*

*In 1992 I went to see the minister then, Fay Chung. I spoke to her about the problem which school children had of not having "A" Level at schools. This problem presented a lot of other problems because children ended up enrolling in Western surburbs. The children would end up begging on the streets because sometimes they would not have enough bus fare and also they would not have carried food to eat. So because of this they would end up begging what we call street begging.*

*When I had realised this I went to see Fay Chung since she is also a woman and was a minister as well. I asked her to look at "A" Level schools on her map in Bulawayo were they were situated. She looked at the map and even looked in Harare as well. She said Mrs. Masuku, 'I did not realise this about "A" Level'. She said that she did not have teachers for "A" Level that year but promised me that the next year she would provide "A" Level teachers at Luveve Secondary. In 1993 we got "A" Level at Luveve Secondary.*

*I can say that was the first thing that people of Luveve will say we got by working with our MP Mrs Masuku.*

*We did a lot of things, because the government was now concentrating in the rural areas. So as parents we needed to find ways to improve our schools.*

*We worked together as parents to make sure that we get the money and resources to improve our schools.*

*The City Council also got involved in helping in various ways and also built laboratories at the schools.*

*Then I realised that there were some students who were not doing well and when they left school they would have problems getting jobs. Especially girls. I then discussed this with the heads of the three schools to see how we could help students who would not have made it academically. We decided to teach them sewing* so that in case they do not make it academically they would have something to help them get jobs. I went to the American Embassy through their project which is called Self Help, and I got 30 machines. I gave ten to each school – 10 for Luveve High, 10 at Nyanda Secondary School. This is some of the work I did when I was MP to help my constituency.

Women showed interest that they wanted to farm paprika. I worked with them and the City Council gave them a place to farm paprika. It is unfortunate that thieves stole their fence but their gardens are still there and they are still farming paprika.

Then I thought of the youth exchange program between Luveve and Sweden. I wanted the young people to go out there and see how other people live and maybe that would inspire them and vice versa.

I would take 8 from Luveve and 8 from Sweden for six months. The youth from Sweden would come and then go back to Sweden with the Luveve youth. I then decided to have it as a national project and there were youths from Gwanda, Harare and Rusape going to Sweden.

## Canaan Jenje (1934 – 1993)

**Canaan (MaDube) Jenje** lived in Mbare and was a member of ZAPU. She used to help school children who did not afford to pay school fees. She would go to the First Lady then Amai Sally Mugabe who would assist through her organisation Child Survival Foundation. Her background as a teacher and later as a journalist made it possible for Mrs. Jenje to knock on doors to ask for help for the township children whose parents could not afford to pay for their fees.

Because of her work in the community she was respected and often elected to positions of leadership. When ZANU PF and PF ZAPU had a unity accord in 1987, Canaan Jenje was elected in absentia to be the Chairperson (Chairman) of ZANU PF of Mbare.

Her understanding of local and international politics impacted on how I view politics and influenced my Pan Africanismness.

# USING MUSIC TO DESTROY COLOUR BAR

# Using music to destroy colour bar – Eileen and Mike Haddon

## Eillen Haddon – (1921 – 2003) | Mike Haddon – (1915 – 1996)

*Eileen Haddon*

**Eileen Haddon** together with her husband Mike Haddon used music to try and bring races together, they tried to destroy colour bar using music. Eileen organized music concerts as a way to bring people of different races together. She would go to the township to look for black musicians to have concerts which included all races. She turned her bedroom into a dancing hall. Haddon used the concerts to raise funds for the multi-racial organisation that she had founded with her husband and multi-racial citizens.

In an interview that I had with **Eileen Haddon** this is what she said:

*We were really involved because we were trying to raise money. At that time we belonged to an outfit called the Inter-racial association. The Inter-racial association was started in the early 50s to try to breakdown the colour bar and to persuade whites that blacks were human beings too. We were always short of money so*

*as part of our fund raising attempt, we tried to put on concerts. There was tremendous interest in Harare and Highfield was just beginning. In music South Africa had been leading the field but we found some good people in Zimbabwe. Alick Nkata who was an employee of the broadcasting and the television and was a very good musician. There was also Moses Mpahlo and the City Quads and Sonny Sondo. We did several things, for example, one year we were trying to persuade whites that it was all right to open restaurants and tearooms to people of all races. After all this was Federation and we were supposed to have a policy of partnership but nothing had happened. We at very short notice were able to hire a stand at the Salisbury show grounds to run what*

*City Quads*

*De Black Evening Follies*

*we called the International restaurant. We ran it for five days when the show was on. We served dinners and lunches and had entertainment at night as well. Much to our surprise we were flooded. We thought that we were going to have maybe one or two liberal whites. Instead, people were queuing outside and we kept running out of food. It was really agonising because one time I had to go and fetch Sonny Sondo in Harare (Mbare) and I could not find him. I had to go driving around these terrible roads asking everyone where Sonny was, until I found him.*

Sonny Sondo was an important person in the music industry, he was leader of the City Quads which worked with Eileen Haddon. Some of the bands that Eileen worked with were the De Black Evening Follies which was led by Moses Mpahlo Mafusire and Alick Nkatha and the All Stars.

*We had another occasion that I would not forget although it is now a long time ago. We had another fund raising concert and we had Indian dancers, African bands and Pat Travers. Pat Travers had the coloureds to contribute too and we sold tickets to V.I.Ps at £5.00 a ticket. They would not have paid that for any other concert but this was done on a social charity basis. We managed to fill the hall although I do not remember what all in all was. There were other people, there was Moses, Pat Travers, the City Quads but I am not sure about Alick Nkata he may well have been. At that time it went down quite well in spite of all the not knowing where the house lights were. I was running around the hall trying to find were the switch was, for the auditorium, the show was on and the lights were still out and nobody knew how to turn them on. Mike Haddon shared his fond memories of those days: The other thing that we did was to get the Jairos Jiri band. I cannot remember what year it was but they came to our Meyrick Park home and played in the garden. It was quite a successful small occasion and we continued to do that.*

Eileen Haddon continued to explain: The funds we were raising, there were simply to keep the organisation going so that we could by example, by precept try and improve the political situation. As far as the race relations were concerned one of the things we used to do, we had committees on labour relations.

Now the government that was during Todd's Premiership had set up a series of commissions to investigate and I was particularly involved in the labour side of things. Two or three of us with Charles Mzingeli who would present evidence to the commission pointing out that the kind of wages people were paid were absolutely ridiculous. People were being paid £5.00 a month, something like that. I remember one particular occasion were I weighed out the amount of maize meal, the amount of maize meal and the amount of sugar and that amount of whatever that you could buy for the whole month's wages. Took it along to the commission to show how impossible it would be for a man to have a wife and two children to live on that with nothing else, no rent, no water, no clothes, to try and persuade them to change it. We did a lot of work on franchise trying to appeal to the commission and the general public. We used to have evening discussions that the franchise should be opened up. We did a bit on housing to try and show that the kind of housing that was being supplied was just not adequate, this kind of stuff.

The Old Bricks had no sanitation, no running water and under the Housing Minister – Jeffrey Almon Brown - a scheme was started to build houses which were going to be sold to people in the townships and we of the Interracial Association took people down to go and have a look at this, we were absolutely applauded. I remember Herbert Chitepo was with us. He was then, I think on the Pullman Commission. He was investigating the whole question of Africans and their living conditions and the whole political scene and we went into the main bedroom.

There were two little rooms and you could not get two single beds into that bedroom and we were complaining that this kind of low level housing was not good enough and people were expecting better things under the Federation. That was the kind of pressure we were doing. I suppose really if you think about it, the Interracial Association was a bit like the FORUM. It was a pressure group. It wasn't a political party.

We were trying to educate the government as well as the people.

# THE 1970'S: THE WELFARE OF THE CHILDREN AND EDUCATION

# The 1970'S
# The Welfare of the Children and Education
# –Thenjiwe Lesabe and Diana Mitchell

## Thenjiwe Lesabe – (1932- 2011) | Diana Mitchell – (1932 – 2006)

The political situation in Zimbabwe became very stressful in the 1970's and it affected black young people's education, some left the country to get the education elsewhere and those who were in the country found it difficult to manoeuvre this situation. Women activists were involved in trying to rectify this situation.

**Thenjiwe Lesabe**

Thenjiwe Lesabe was one of the women who had the welfare of young people at heart and in the 1970's, she organized scholarships for many to go and study abroad while she was in exile in Botswana. Many young people benefitted from the scholarships that she ogarnised. One of those who benefitted from the scholarships is Emanuel Jenje – brother of the author of this book – *History of Women Politicians of Zimbabwe*. Emmanuel left for

*Emmanuel Jenje*

Botswana on a visitor's visa and when he got to Botswana he stayed at a camp were Thenjiwe Lesabe organized for him to go to the United States to study at the University of California.

A nationalist, Freedom fighter, teacher and journalist. Thenjiwe resigned from teaching in 1949 to become a journalist with the *Bantu Mirror*. She started her political activism the year she became a journalist in Bulawayo. Lesabe became a member of Gama Sigma which was composed of people who had various interests including intellectuals, community well-being issues which included education for Africans were also discussed and implemented. Gama Sigma was comprised of experts who mapped the people's liberation's struggle.

Thenjiwe Lesabe was one of the first people to join the Southern Rhodesia African National Congress in 1957.

Lesabe worked to form a branch called MZIBA (Mzilikazi/Barbourfields) by mobilizing and conscientising people in Mzilikazi and Babourfields and formed a branch known as MZIBA (Mzilikazi/Babourfields). She was the leader of the Zapu women's league, ZAWU, until the party was banned in 1962.

At the height of the clampdown on the leadership of the nationalist movement by the Ian Smith regime, in 1978 Lesabe went into exile. She helped send many young people to school all over the world and also helped with the training of exiles in camps.

When Zimbabwe attained its independence she held a number of posts as ZAPU, ZANU PF and at National level.

Born at Hope Fountain near Bulawayo on 5 January 1932, Lesabe died in 2011 and was denied hero status despite all the work she did for the country, but she was given state funeral. This raised the question – Who is supposed to be buried at the Heroes Acre?

## Diana Mitchell

Diana Mitchell became a political activist and tried to correct the political imbalances through her work, she earned herself the title of *Ambuya* Diana (Grandmother Diana). Mitchell fought hard to have some black children be able to go to school and

today she is an *ambuya* (grandmother) to many children whom she helped to educate during UDI. Black children and White children did not go to school together. The children of Black domestic workers in the affluent white areas were bused to schools in Black townships. In protest, Diana Mitchell, who was then Chairperson of the friends of African children, used to go door to door in the affluent white areas raising money and clothes to educate Black children. One of the children she helped to get education during UDI was John Indi who later became involved in theatre, film and he is an entrepreneur. Diana used to ask the rich white residents: *"How can you let these children live in your backyard, the most expensive areas of the country, and deny them schooling?"* It was through this protest that she was groomed to be a politician. Diana Mitchel was for 15 years Press and Public Relations Officer for the Center Party which fought Ian Smith's UDI.

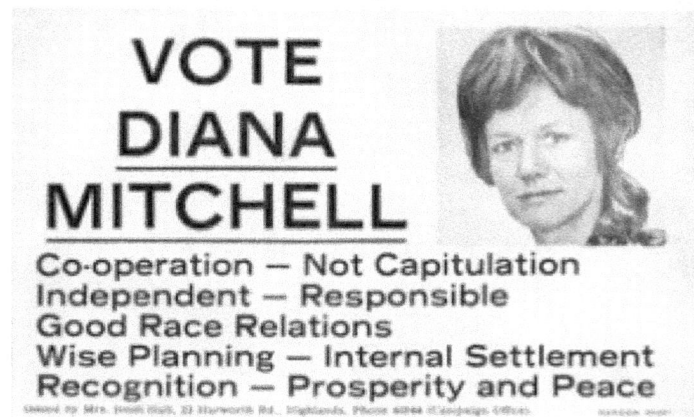

## VOTE DIANA MITCHELL

Co-operation — Not Capitulation
Independent — Responsible
Good Race Relations
Wise Planning — Internal Settlement
Recognition — Prosperity and Peace

Diana Mitchel gives us an insight on how the political situation during the Federation and UDI impacted on black children. She also re-counts how she was involved in helping black children get education.

*You could say education was Federal so it was the economy of scale. So there could be a spill off effect there. But once UDI came you can imagine? That is what I was saying earlier and they took a step backwards. Education was affected.*

*Once UDI was declared in 1965 it overlooked the fact that we had a population ....which my memory could not return everything but I know that we were out numbered 100 to 1 by black people and it seemed foolish no matter what your political view. No matter you were a racist or you were a hair longed liberal. No matter which perspective. The fact is we were living in*

*an African country in which Africans were outnumbering whites to 100 – 1, and you were telling Africans that there were second class citizens, that they should take second place, it could not have worked.*

It was because of the political situation which discriminated on black people hence affecting the education of black children that turned Diana Mitchell into an activist. She worked hard to see to it that black children got decent education.

*It was my part in educating the black children – John Indi you mentioned. His parents lived in this area and the Rhodesian Front Government could not let black children be educated. The Rhodesian Front Policy would not let black children be educated in white areas and so to cut a long story short - The Rhodesian Front bulldozed schools, the Forestry Commission had a school and John*

**Diana Mitchell with John Indi**

Indi was one of the people at the school bulldozed and his parents were not able to send him to the township schools because of cost of transport. They were not rich people, it was out of their reach and children were sitting at the backyard of Highlands. It was an exclusive area and there were not able to be educated. I went to beg a minister of government to look at this policy, in my innocence. I thought if I appeal to this minister to say look at what you are doing, you are creating malcontents and your children go to school in Mercedes Benz.

Black children had no chance. Mrs. Holdersness, she set up a kind of school in her own environment, it seems to us we were not allowed to have schools in our backyards to help these children. But all we could do is to raise funds to send them to mission schools. That is what we did. We formed a committee. Those backyard schools were bulldozed. I was pulled in by her (Mrs Holderness) and we formed the Friends of African Children. That was great injustice of myself having had good education and seeing the children of people who had made my life here could not go to school. It did not make sense.

So that is what got me asking the minister to say can you not provide schools for these children in Highlands, can you not even allow them to go to Epworth. The answer by the Rhodesian minster was "That is government policy". That made me understand the word policy for the first time.

It seemed to me the only way to counter it was to have a different government with a different policy. That is when I joined in with the opposition politics.

Well those days it was not too difficult we had a residue of the Federation. Let's call them White Liberals. For the sake of short hand. White Liberals are now despised, I am sorry to say. But in my own experience there were the whites who could have made this if the federation could have been governed by the sort of those people, maybe I might be wrong. Those whites understood – disadvantages of those children and we went and collected money for them. They came here, in this drive way, the poor and the rich.

A widow came with ten shillings saying this is the money to help the children. So we raised funds as a committee and we were able to travel. I had a kombi and 10 children in it and I drove out to Chivero. There was a school there and the headmaster ….and I asked him please admit 10 children that I had come with. He took them. I got home late that night my husband was furious because he thought I had gone missing. That is what we did. We sent children to mission schools, where ever we could find places. We sent them to mission/boarding schools by bus or by train.

# The Liberation War and Women – Political Situation was Becoming Unbearable

During the 1970's the political situation continued to become unbearable and many women got involved in the liberations struggle to free their country from oppression, the liberation war saw both men and women taking up arms to fight colonial rule. Some of the women who joined the liberation struggle are Jane Ngwenya, Eunice Nomthandazo Sandi Moyo, Thenjiwe Lesabe, Angeline Masuku, Chiratidzo Iris Mabuwa, Oppah Muchinguri, Margaret Dongo, Sithabile Sibanda, Freedom Nyamubaya, Monica Mutsvangwa, Joyce Fortune Dube, Sibonokuhle Moyo (Getrude Mpala), Noma Tshuma (Georgina Mabhena) Dadirai Njitimana and Tsitsi Kahari.

Although many women joined the struggle under ZANLA and ZIPRA, very few were rewarded after the war, when they were expected to assume the "woman's role". Reintegrating into the community was a double jeopardy. The society did not accept them as "women", and they found themselves working twice harder than the "ordinary" woman would do, so as to be accepted in the society. Some lost themselves in the process and became more subservient than their counterparts who did not take up arms in the war. Many families would not approve of their son marrying an ex-combatant for a wife. Some of the women that I have spoken to find it very difficult to talk about their experiences both during and after the war, and sometimes wonder why they even went to war.

**Jane Ngwenya**, under the ZIPRA wing command, was the first woman to take up arms and go into the bush to fight. She however regretted why she ever

*Jane Ngwenya*

fought in the liberation war as no one seemed to recognize the contributions she made and others of her time. *Jane Ngwenya spent most of her years in politics, which saw her losing her marriage, as her husband became jealous that she was sometimes the only woman in a meeting full of men. She also gave up her teaching career as she was outspoken about the way the teachers were paid compared to their white counterparts. She was to spend 9 years in solitary confinement* in Hwahwa and Gonakudzingwa Prisons. "There are times when I regret why I ever fought for this country. No-one seems to remember or to recognize that sacrifice. The fact of the matter is we could not all become ministers but the political set-up is all wrong." Said Jane Ngwenya in an interview with Nelson Chenga –Herald.

Ngwenya joined the African National Congress in 1959. The following year she became a national council member of National Democratic Party. The NDP was banned on December 9, 1961 and ZAPU was launched 10 days later, with just about the same leadership. Ngwenya was appointed national secretary for women's affairs. Between 1964 and 1971 she was detained at the notorious Hwahwa and Gonakudzingwa. Her appetite for fighting white rule grew even stronger while in detention. At Hwahwa she was thrown into solitary confinement as punishment for inciting other women prisoners to challenge poor conditions in jail. She said, wet and cold conditions in jail resulted in her developing arthritis that has now worsened with age. She escaped to Zambia where she was based in Lusaka under the Zimbabwe African People's Union and was responsible for the welfare of freedom fighters in operational zones. While in Lusaka she was seriously burned in a parcel bomb blast that killed the Zapu military leader Jason 'Ziyapapa' Moyo on January 22 1977. She was elected to Parliament on PF- Zapu ticket in 1980, representing Matabeleland North.

As one among the many women, who participated in the war of liberation, Ngwenya is concerned that deeply ingrained tradition still affects the rights of women in general. "The Government is trying to recognize us, not that it likes us, but because we fought to be recognized", she said. (Nelson Chenga – The Herald – June 10, 1999).

Ngwenya served as Deputy Minister of Labor, Manpower and Social Protection during Zimbabwe's first independent government in 1980.
Jane Ngwenya was born on the 15th June 1935. She died in Bulawayo on 5 August 2021 at the age of 86 and was buried at the Zimbabwe National Heroes Acre in Harare as she was declared a national heroin.

## Eunice Nomthandazo Sandi Moyo

Many more women followed in the steps of Jane Ngwenya and joined the struggle. One of the women was Eunice Sandi Nomthandazo Sandi Moyo.

**Eunice Sandi Moyo**

**Eunice Nomthandzo Sandi Moyo** started politics when she was very young in South Africa where she lived with her parents in Soweto - Alexander. Her father was from Zimbabwe and her mother from South Africa. When she got into politics her father was very worried and he was a policemen who was supposed to arrest those who were against the Apartheid government, but this did not deter Eunice Nomthandazo. The injustices by the Apartheid regime in South Africa gave her no choice but to challenge the system. She was later arrested but was not sent to Robin Island like the others because she was still at school.

In that process we ended up not being arrested and being sent to Robin Island like the others. We remained because we were going to school but we were going to be monitored until we finished school. But one day my father decided. 'I think you should go home you are becoming a problem.' So I was brought here in Zimbabwe."

Sandi Moyo narrates how she left the country to go

overseas and eventually to Zambia, were she trained as a liberation fighter. She also describes how the Rhodesian government killed people in Zambia at the refugee and training camps.

*Someone was sent to come and give us tickets. We were 10 when we left. I was the only girl with 9 guys we took a train and went to Botswana, when we got to Botswana we were detained by the police and we were kept there for a day and then the following day we were taken to where the refugees were kept and we were taken from there to go to Zambia because, the plan was that we go to school. We were not really going there to be trained. We were supposed to go to school. Yes we went to school, some went to Germany and some went to Denmark.*

*It was very difficult for us to come back home because the authorities were looking for us. So we stayed (in Zambia). So we were mandated to be trained cadres because it was very unsafe not to be a trained person. Because if an attack comes, how are you going to protect yourself. So we stayed. I was staying with umama uJane Ngwenya, when mama Lesabe arrived I was already there, Mama Mrs Dhlomo who came from Midlands, found me there. Mama Nyamurova she also found me there. You are trained to be able to use the gun. You are also trained war tactics when you confront an enemy. How to look after your gun. But in most cases, they did not give ammunition. They could give us guns to keep, if there was an attack, then you were given ammunition. But as for me, I never experienced an attack.*

*Attacks were at Nkoma camp when I had left. We went to look for those who had been attacked. Smith's army used to come they attacked the FC, which was just for the boys who were being trained there. A lot of them died there, but some managed to escape, and they went into the bush. This other camp, which was for girls called Mkushi there was also a massacre. There was a massacre! It was very, very painful. I am one of those who went out with cars going to look for them. Some had run away, because when they left the country they went to Botswana and then they were moved from Botswana and were taken to camps in Zambia. They didn't even know where they were. So when they were trying to escape, they did not know where they were going. They were in the dark just running, not knowing where they were going, they were all over the Bush.*

*So we started looking for them. Let me tell you ...when you found them in trees and asked them to climb down, you know there were wild, there were scared to climb down the trees because Smith's soldiers had come with people who could speak Ndebele and Shona who were telling them to climb down and promised that there were not going to kill them and would say, the whites have gone. They spoke in Shona and Ndebele, and they would come down from the trees, and they would be shot. That is what happened. So they didn't trust anyone moreover we were using camouflaged cars because all war cars are camouflaged. They did not trust that we were genuine they thought we were those people who wanted to kill them. Even if we assured them that we have not come to fight with you (them). 'Look, we do not have any guns'. They were scared because they were not sure that even if we were not armed, but who else could be out there in the bush waiting for them. Well, we managed to rescue some, and the others had gone up as far as to the Zambezi River, and their feet were damaged, and they could not walk. But that was the story which was very painful in Mkushi. At FC yes because those were killed but some of them escaped into the city because FC was near the suburbs, but Mkushi was in the bush. It was very painful. That is why I get hurt when some people claim that there were in the war of liberation- and yet there were not. It's very painful.*

Eunice Sandi Moyo encourages other women to be in politics and why it is vital that women become part of the country's politics.

*It's good for women to venture into politics because politics decides the way a country should go, so women must be part of that decision-making process, but unfortunately sometimes personal egos hamper this set-up. We sometimes become too greedy, sometimes we want to challenge each other over nothing. I believe we should focus with the agenda of promoting women in the manner that it should be, the manner is don't challenge a woman who is already in a position, get the positions that the men are holding so that you become more in the set-up. What is the point of having 10 women out of 160 men, it does not work, then you go there and you fight for those 10 posts." Advice from Sandi Moyo a veteran politician whose political career spans 5 decades. She surely knows what she is saying.*

"Women must focus on what women need; women need power to bring up their children, to bring up the nation, women need power to bring economics into the country to make other women rich. Riches must not belong to men only, but to women also. I would encourage women never to give up, this is a long struggle, and we still have a long way to go. We have to even convince our children, our boys, not to stop them from doing household chores and say they are for girls. Make children feel that they are the same, they are at the same level. My kids, I have one boy, he does all those even now at the age of 35 because when he married he married a partner in everything he does"

Sandi Moyo was born in Zimbabwe in 1946 but grew up in South Africa, where she trained as a teacher. She returned to teach in Zimbabwe in 1960, and joined ZAPU. She went to Zambia in 1975 where she trained as a soldier, and was sent to Germany to train in reconnaissance. She was a broadcaster for ZAPU. In 1988 she set up a book selling business, Z and N, with Zodwa Sibanda (the wife of late Gibson Sibanda). She worked in Nkomo's office after independence, and was a politburo member for ZANU PF, and the Deputy Chairperson for Women's League. She became Senator of Plumtree Constituency from 2006-2008. She is the former Minister of State for Bulawayo Metropolitan Province. She wants to see more women, more so young women involved in mainstream politics. She encourages women to strategise in order to have their space in the political arena.

**Eunice Sandi Moyo with Theresa Makone (left) and Tandiwe Mlilo (right)**

# The Younger Generation of 1970's and the Struggle

While the younger generation in the 1970's was going about their lives they realized that, that was not the kind of life they deserved. As young people music was one of their pass time and in the 1970's rock was one avenue to vent their anger since rock music was revolutionary in nature. The rock culture wanted to change almost everything in the world including politics. A song like Calling Your Name was composed as a result of young people who were leaving the country to go and fight. You would look for your friend in places that you were used to find them but they were gone. You would call their name but they were far away.

A number of young people both male and female, in the urban and rural left to join the struggle.

## JOYCE MUJURU

Joyce Mujuru is one of the few women who was in the liberation struggle in the 1970's who has held the highest position in the government, that of being vice president. In 1973, Joice Mujuru left the country to join the liberation struggle, where she rose through the ranks of Zanla, the armed wing of Zanu (PF). She became medical assistant, then military commander and Central Committee member. She has held different posts since independence in 1980. At independence some women were appointed as ministers, although very few got full ministerial positions. Mujuru was Minister of Youth, Sports and Recreation. Most of the women assumed positions of deputies. Amongst the women ministers' were, Naomi Nhiwatiwa and Victoria Chitepo who was the Deputy Minister of Education and Culture and Naome Nhiwatiwa became Deputy Minister of Post and Telecommunications.

**Joice Mujuru and Victoria Chitepo**

## NAOMI NHIWATIWA

Joice Mujuru (nom de guerre *Teurai Ropa)* was one of the few women who were appointed as full ministers.

As a Minister of Women Affairs, she lobbied for the Legal Majority Act 1992, which opened doors for women to be able to take decisions without men. Joice Mujuru continued to encourage women to fight for their rights, and also encouraged them to join trade unions. She remains the highest ranking woman in Zimbabwe politics, the first woman to attain a high post in government as the vice president of the country. Joice Mujuru was the Minister of Community Development and Women's Affairs at the attainment of Zimbabwe's independence in 1980.

At a Women's Day rally on March 8, 1983, Joice Mujuru also known by her Chimurenga name *Teurai Ropa Nhongo,* urged women to press for their rights.

She told the meeting that the goal of Zimbabwe as a developing socialist state was equality for all citizens before the law.

She said - *Women participated in the national liberation struggle for human rights, and their resources must be made full use of in a mutually complementary manner, rather than in a master-servant relationship, which smacks of exploitation of one group by the other?*

On that same occasion, she urged women to join trade unions. Women, she said, could do as well as men if they were only given the chance.

But she pointed out that in Harare out of 86 councilors, only two were women, and Bulawayo had none. In Parliament, the body that represents the whole society, there were only 12 women out of 140.

She pointed out, too, that although the Government was the largest employer of labour, no woman yet sat on the Public Services Commission.

*"These are the areas we need to transform,"* she said. (Weiss 1986, 23)

The demands for women's rights from almost all quarters of society including the highest echelons were growing.

Joice Mujuru held different posts in Government before she became Vice President on December 6, 2004.

In 1985 she became Minister of State up to 1988. She then became Minister of Community Development, Cooperatives and Women's Affairs up to 1992.

She was Governor and Resident Minister of Mashonaland Central Province up to 1996.

*Joyce Mujuru*

She also served as the Minister of Information, Posts and Telecommunications for a year, and in 1997 she was assigned Minister of Rural Resources and Water Development up to 2004 when she was appointed Vice President. However in 2014 she was accused of plotting against Mugabe. She lost both her post as Vice-President and her position in the party leadership. She later on formed her party - Zimbabwe People First party, which is now defunct.

## MARGARET DONGO

One woman ex-combatant who changed the terrain of post-independence Zimbabwean politics is Margaret Dongo (nom de guerre Tichaona Muhondo). She refused to give up her fighting spirit, she became the first ever woman independent MP in Zimbabwe and she was standing for Sunningdale. She served as a parliamentarian for many years later founding the Zimbabwe Union for Democrats – ZUD in 1998, the only political party headed by a female then. Believing in women economic empowerment, Marga-

ret Dongo engineered a lot of self-help projects for women during her tenure as a member of parliament for Sunningdale. She educated people in her constituency on their rights and her constituency Harare South was dubbed the 'Republic'. She explained the caliber of women in her constituency in an interview I had with her in the 90's. *Women in my constituency are quite different from women of other constituencies. They are not the so-called intellectuals or academics who at times don't even know their rights, despite the fact that they are in advantageous positions. Some women in my constituency have never gone to school. But when they stand up to tell you their rights, their role as women, and their role as citizens of Zimbabwe, you feel proud.*

She has not been afraid to challenge structures particularly those which oppress women and children. In 2010 she challenged the traditional set up regarding inheritance. The rural areas sometimes make it difficult for women to voice their concerns as regards inheritance, as far as traditional law is concerned the home belongs to the males of the family. A woman was chased away from her home in Mhondoro rural by her in-laws, after her husband and son had died, Margaret intervened and she was brought back to her village - homestead.

Margaret Dongo has been a trailblazer in many ways she co-founded together with a few other freedom fighters, the National Liberation War Veterans Association, designed to champion the cause of demobilized ex-combatants who had become destitute? In 1990 when Dongo was elected a ZANU-PF member of parliament. She quickly pushed for a war veteran's administration bill.

Margaret Dongo fought single handedly in Parliament to stop some bills from becoming law. At one time a male parliamentarian threatened to beat her up when he felt challenged.

Dongo threatened to slide on Shamuyarira's bold forehead, and this saw some cartoonists coming up with cartoons which were very incensitive. For instance there was a cartoon which showed Margaret sliding on Shamuyarira without a panty. It was in very bad test.

She also challenged the Registrar General that women could also acquire passports for their children without their husbands as husbands were allowed to acquire passports for the children without

*Margaret Dongo holding a brochure explaining a woman as a legal guidian to her child just like the men*

their wives. This meant that a woman was an equal guardian just like the men.

When Margaret Dongo attempted to retain her seat in the 2000 election, her house was attacked by a group of 60 opponents who threw rocks through the windows. She lost the elections, but continues to fight for women's rights. Now based in Mhondoro, she continues with her activism work and she has helped a number of people particularly women to understand their rights.

**But how did Margaret become political conscious and joined the liberation struggle? She takes us through her journey.**

Right when I was fifteen (fifteen) years is when I joined the Liberation Struggle. In fact one thing I am happy about, I was not recruited by anyone. I took an initiative on my own, this is why you find that I am so independent. I don't belong to individuals. Nobody can tell me to say, it's me who recruited you from school. In fact what I can say is that my family was highly political. I must have inherited it from my family. Because I had a situation where I had my mother supporting UP because she was a Methodist and she believed in Muzorewa very much. And a situation where my father coming from Chipinge and grew up with Ndabaningi and he was supporting Sithole.

I had a situation where when I was growing up there used to be these debates which led me, I realised that at the end of the day to say these people are making sense probably in all the discussions they used to hold. This is what made me join the Liberation Struggle and I became ZANU. And I re-

member my father before he died, he used to say, Margaret one day if God will keep me alive, one day you are going to be opposition and I used to deny because I believed in ZANU PF. Nobody would talk ill about ZANU PF, you know when I was still coming from the war. And I would say to my mother and father, you are lost, I am not visiting you because of your silly comments that you make and all he would say is, 'Margaret I wish God would see me through. One day you will be opposition' but it's unfortunate that they died before I became opposition.

**So you can say you were brought up in this family which was political conscious?**

Yes, Yes. It's something that I grew up in. Politics you know has become part of my life and a lot of people were saying to me when I lost my seat. Everyone was coming to me to say – What are you going to do now that you have lost your seat in parliament. And I said parliament was not the end of my life, it was a platform which I would use to put whatever ideas that I had.

The time that I was in parliament do you know that we were earning about 8,000 Zimbabwean dollars a month for the past 10 years that we have been in parliament? That would mean for us it was all about commitment. It was not about money and still today it has become part of my hobby and so this is why I have continued with politics.

# ZIMBABWE RHODESIA TO ZIMBABWE

# Zimbabwe Rhodesia to Zimbabwe – and Women after the War and Independence

While the Liberation War was going on in order to free Zimbabwe, a kind of settlement was also going on in the country and this was between Ian Smith and Abel Muzorewa. The name of the country got a double barrel name, and it was called Zimbabwe – Rhodesia. It was hard to name the country as there was no one with full control. However in this confusion blackwomen managed to be in politcs and some of them were Joyce Nxahe, Joyce Chenzira Mutasa, Vesta Saungweme, Ester Mhembere, Vishet Dziruni and Poshi Mugudubi.

While all this was happening the liberation war was taking place and it had escalated. In 1980, the country celebrated independence and like everyone else women were overjoyed. But this was going to be short lived as women's efforts during the war were not recognized. Women were taken back to being 'women' and became second class citizens in the country they fought for.

Margaret Dongo who took part in the liberation war clarifies this situation.

**Ester Mhembere**

**Vesta Saungweme**

**Poshi Mugudubi**

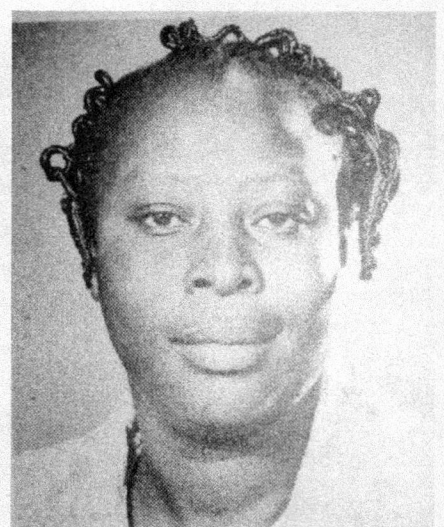

**Joyce Nxahe**

**Joyce Chenzira Mutasa**

**Vishet Dziruni**

## Margaret Dongo

*Women in Zimbabwe, women in the whole world, we don't have space at all. We have not yet created our space. We are just like dependents and we need to fight for it. The reason I am saying this, you find that a lot of governments have signed a lot of conversions – the CEDAW and all that but they have not domesticated them. The reason why they have not domesticated them is that they have not effected them. They have not implemented them.*

*The reason being that they still undermine the role that is played by women to some extent but what they do, they know that women are very good organisers at the grassroots level. All the man who come into power, they are put into power by women to some extent, by the poor women. But when it comes to sharing the piece of cake you find that that's when women are set aside. Even if you look at our background, the women who have been in the liberation struggle, we fought side by side men, we endured much more hardships than these men.*

*You know when you are still a teenager you go through your stages of maturity, a lot of things happen but some of those things you could live with them but still*

**Margaret Dongo**

*doing our usual tasks. But at the end of the day you talk about our history after independence, what happened – women went into the background.*

# WOMEN AND POLITICAL VIOLENCE

# Women and Political Violence

While women are doing everything they can in order to be in mainstream politics, they are faced with stumbling blocks which makes it impossible for them to attain the highest decision making body in the country. Amongst other obstacles political violence plays a major role in blocking women's participation in politics.

However women have continued to fight to be part of the highest decision making body in the land – politics. Political violence has disenfranchised women thereby closing the political space for them. This is because of their vulnerable position in the society.

Women politicians in Zimbabwe have been facing violence in all forms – physically, emotionally and sexually. Women's sexuality and everything to do with their biological make up is battered in order to deter women from attaining the highest office in the land were decisions are made. The abuse is accelerated towards and during campaigning for elections and after the elections. A number of aspiring women politicians have dropped out of elections because of violence. But some have faced it head on. Women politicians discuss the political terrain they have travelled and how violence has made it difficult for women to operate freely as full citizens.

## RUTH CHINAMANO

Ruth Chinamano explains the political violence she faced during elections.

*If it wouldn't have been for Mugabe I wouldn't have been a member of parliament. They made me to stand with Mugabe and I was nearly killed. The women were*

*Ruth Chinamano*

*going with baskets saying, "Tirikuta (tirikuda) musoro wake, tirikuta musoro wake." (We want her head. We want her head?).*

**Joyce - But how do you see yourself after independence, can you say you have achieved what you fought for?**

*What I have achieved is very little. I gave my whole self to liberate Zimbabwe from the white rule and from slavery. I didn't have time with my children. I was busy sleeping in Lupane, I was busy sleeping in UMtali. We*

**Betty Mtero and Victoria Chitepo**

were all over.


## BETTY MTERO
Betty Mtero on women politicians and violence:

### Joyce - Why do you think they use violence to campaign – the politicians?

Well because they fail to think for themselves. You know they can't reason. For instance if some members of the opposition came to me, I would rather sit down and discuss to convince that person why I don't support their party and I don't support whatever it is. I will really sit and talk, I believe people should have dialogue. If I want you to join my part and I know you belong to another party, the best thing is I will visit you, talk to you, and tell you all about my party, all policies and so forth rather than fighting with you. So its lack of understanding in the people, which is a problem.

In 2000, Betty Mutero dropped out of the parliamentary election race in order to protect her dignity.

I don't want to end up running in the township lifting my dress or without a dress at all [naked], because of violence, I want to keep my dignity

She saw how some male politicians used money to buy votes by taking advantage of the desperate situations of women in the townships, and also buying beer for the youths who would in turn become violent and attack political opponents. Betty, who was a ZANU PF candidate, said she could not corrupt and turn the youths into hooligans by buying them beer, the very same people that she would like to lead, so she decided she would watch the race from a distant.

### Joyce - You have dropped twice from the MP race?

Oh MP race, you know what I have observed is that especially with women there is need for political education so that women have to make their own decision, they must really get to know what politics is. What is the role of women in politics? Because women still; think that they are represented better by man than by women, so if one has to be their candidate as a woman you really have to go out of your way and work very hard as I said earlier on that when I first contested in Bulawayo for the position of Board Member (Councillor), there was no campaigning were actually people had to use money as such but I found that you know now the pattern is that of money, which is really called vote buying. If it were money spent on organizing workshops to educate women on how to vote and who to vote for and how to support other women then I will be happy.

## MARGARET DONGO

**Margaret Dongo** on her experience on political violence.

*What I experience in 1995 – I had a situation where you would find people phoning my husband during the election campaigns. I am out campaigning, of course you campaign as late and you have sleepless nights. You know that's the time politicians don't sleep because every time you are on the planning board to see what is going to happen tomorrow. So you find someone phoning him (husband), I remember my husband going to court. He used to be phoned in by my opponents to say your wife is going around and is bit…..ng around, and you know by so doing they want to give you double pressure. So that you have pressure in the house, you have pressure outside so that you give in the pol-*itics. *But anywhere thank heaven that I had a strong independent husband who was actually very supportive. So all he did he took me by surprise and he took some of the guys to court and said it's insulting, you are tarnishing the image of my wife. She has her own right to participate in politics the way she likes. If I can communicate with other people, why not my wife. In any case she is supposed to extend her association better than me because she is in politics so I am very happy that I had a supportive husband.*

*To some extent my children were affected. One day they were taken out. I had some Swedish friends and they came on holidays and they said Margaret …. Because I had a series of attacks at home. So they said Margaret it will put your kids in a very difficult position and they are still growing up. We want to take your kids out for lunch. So they drove out. So they said it so happened that their radio was on and there was a report, you know somebody was reporting that there has been violence in Sunningdale and this is what has happened. Margaret Dongo's house has been attacked and they had to switch off the radio because they had realised that the kids were paying attention. They were beginning to ask. Is that not our mother? Please open loudly we want to hear the story and they closed and they said from there, what they told me was their faces were changed and they were so depressed. So they drove and took them out for lunch but they couldn't have the lunch. They said no, why you don't take us back home, we want to go and see our mother because we hear something on the news.*

*Margaret's friends said - no it's just something which was reported yesterday and they are still carrying out the report. And they said no, we want to go there. But later on the one thing I am happy about my kids, I am happy my kids got used to it. I remember the last time my son had a birthday, so I didn't have time to go and support him so I sent him some goodies and a video. I couldn't believe it, in that video my little sons were talking to these kids and saying vote for my mother.*

## DIANA MITCHELL

It seems in each era women face political violence and this includes their families and their children become vulnerable. **Diana Mitchell's** child faced abuse from a teacher because of her mother's political preference. Diana went back to that time and she takes us through what she went through and her child:

*We were harassed in the sense that we were scorned. My children at school had to face teachers who supported the regime who gave them to understand that their mother was something very peculiar. I had to change schools for my youngest child because he was being harassed by a teacher and I moved him out of the school. We were regarded as being treacherous to our own race. All we wanted was to have a quality of opportunity in your own country. We were treated as Communists as if we were traitors to our own race. Why we were on top we wanted to bring us down?*

## MAVIS CHIDZONGA 1953 - 2011

Many women politicians have walked this path of political violence. **Mavis Chidzonga** takes us through the violence women politicians go through.

The late Mavis Chidzonga a ZANU PF candidate and MP for Mhondoro (1995-2000), was a victim of violence, she said that the violence starts in parliament where women are intimidated, humiliated and silenced, sometimes the whole saga turning to physical abuse when the male politicians feel challenged by women. Mavis explained her experience in parliament.

*To survive in that environment one has to either just give in and sit back and not take part in a number of activities then you are a good girl, then you are alright. Males feel threatened by your presence or if you happen to bring out according to them anything that is* intellectually threatening. For example on my part the first time that I spoke in parliament, I responded to the President's speech and I seconded the motion made by Hounourable Mataure, eeh, phones rang that evening throughout Harare. Men were phoning each other saying have you seen this new breed which has come from Mashonaland West? There was already fear that I was a threat to some men and I didn't realise it, they were phoning each other saying this should not come from a woman.

*Working with the grassroots made it easy for Mavis to know how to respond to issues that were being discussed. I had researched my response, I had brought the issue from the grassroots. I had gone through my constituency so even though it was my three weeks of parliament I had gotten enough information about the whole of my constituency. I brought in well researched issues and real issues that were coming from the people, this apparently had happened rarely, most of the speeches were mediocre type of speeches. I was commended by the speaker that 'it's one of the speeches that we have had in the last parliament, that it is very good.' When it was lunchtime they were comments, you know things like its coming from a woman, who wrote the speech for you it must have been a man you know it's just too good to have been written by a woman.*

The abuse of women in parliament can turn into violence if some male parliamentarians feel challenged. Mavis gave a very interesting example regarding violence perpetrated to women parliamentarians.

*I would actually like to take it to a smaller level for example in a house, in a family if you find a man beating up his wife it is a sign of weakness, not for the woman but for the man who decides that the only way to convince or to control the woman is by beating her up. The issue here is he can't discuss issues with the woman. He can't. If the woman is strong enough to want to communicate with the husband if he can't handle her intelligence then he resorts to violence. So I see this as a method used by politicians, if they can't handle their opponent male or female they resort to violence because they think if we put fear in this person and their supporters, then we will win the election but that's not the good method of winning elections. People should be able to be free to campaign, free to challenge each other on the platform and bring out real issues that matter to the people that would actually help a developing country like ours not to resort to forcing people. You might force them into the ballot box but you are not solving the problems of the country.*

Mavis Chidzonga lost the 2000 elections by a small margin, she was running on a Zanu PF ticket. She was hurt by losing because she had some projects going with The Children of Mhondoro in building the road to Mhondoro.

She felt male and females in Zimbabwe are not ready to have female leaders: You can't change people's minds who have had scuds and scuds of beer for months or presents of machines from male counterparts. She charged. (scud - is opaque beer which is popular with people who drink beer).

Mavis passed away in 2011. She was 58 years old.

## PRSICILLA MISIHAIRABWI MUSHONGA

**Priscilla Misihairabwi-Mushonga**, an outspoken MDC T, parliamentarian (2000-2008) (2008- [MDC N]) spoke of some of the problems she encountered when campaigning in 2000. *I ran into a police station for sanctuary when some rowdy youths wanted to beat me, only to be told that I could not stay in the police station as the station would be stoned!*

Priscilla discouraged violence regardless of the circumstances and advocated for an atmosphere in which people could vote without fear of retribution. Unfortunately, the victims of this violence were often women, who faced difficulties reporting incidents to the authorities and were not given adequate media coverage.

*The same issue with cases of rape, a lot of sexual abuse happening and we know how it is with sexual abuse and women coming out and saying you know I've been sexually abused not many women can actually do that.*

Despite the problems that Priscilla faced during campaigning she was elected MP for Glen Norah in 2000.

During her time as Glen Norah's MP, she also served as the shadow foreign minister for the Movement for Democratic Change. When the party split in 2005, she remained with the MDC formation, and was elected Deputy Secretary-General of that party. She repre-sented her party in the Zimbabwean political nego-tiations.

In 2009 she was appointed Minister of Regional Integration and International Cooperation, in the Government of National Unity. In the 2011 MDC congress she was elected the party' Secretary General a posi-tion she held up to 2016. She was the MDC chief rep-resentative at JOMIC (Joint Monitorinng and Imple-metation Committee) and COPAC the (Constitutional Parliamentary Committee) a committee which was in charge of writing the Zimbabwean constitution. She was also the only female negotiator in the GPA (Global Political Agreement). Priscilla Misihayirabwi Mushonga is now the Ambassador of Zimbabwe to the Kingdom of Sweden.

## THOKOZANI KHUPE

During the same year (2000) **Thokozani Khupe**, a former trade unionist and Deputy President of MDC Tsvangirayi, then Deputy Priminister of Zimbabwe was also attacked while campaigning. A trade unionist, Thokozani Khupe became Deputy Prime Minister of Zimbabwe in 2009. Her political history is entrenched in the Labour Movement.

Could she have heeded to the call by then Minister of Community Development and Women's Affairs, Joice Mujuru who encouraged women to join trade unions in 1983?

Thokozani Khupe served in the Zimbabwe Amalgamated Railway Union (ZARU) in 1987.

In 1991 she was elected Secretary for the ZCTU Women's Advisory Council and also a General Council member of the ZCTU. In 1999 she participated in the formation of the Movement for Democratic Change party, in which she was elected as a National Executive member responsible for Transport, Logis-

tics and Welfare.

In June 2000, she was elected Member of Parliament for Makokoba Constituency in Bulawayo. Thokozani Khupe was the Deputy Prime Minister of the Government of National Unity since February 11, 2009 to 2013.

She was also the Vice President of the Movement for Democratic Change (MDC-T) which she represented in Parliament.

She does not apologies for articulating women's rights, at the re-launch of 50/50

Representation she encouraged women not to adopt the constitution if they were not well represented.

*That constitution must have that provision which says that we need 50% representation of women in all decision-making bodies. It must be there and it must be very, very clear, we don't want any ambiguity, it must be very clear, over and above that we need a close which will clearly state that any political party which does not comply, must be automatically disqualified from that election.*

She charged, and advised women to stop being crying babies.

*We constitute 52% of the population so there is no way we can continue crying, screaming and shouting that no we are not represented equally, no we are being short-changed, no ladies, let's do away with this victim mentality. Let's do away with this cry baby mentality. Let's stand up and stand on our two feet. Let's start fighting for ourselves. We are many we can make it!*

# Strategies and solutions

While violence has been cited as a stumbling block for women to achieving their dreams as leaders in politics, **Monica Mutsvangwa** says that, it is only women themselves who will change this. She advices women to educate men and help to take away the fear in men which has to do with seeing women as mothers and they are scared that once they are in parliament they will 'control' them. Men feel that the space in the home is controlled by women so they have made sure that the space outside the home is theirs and will make sure that they keep it away from women.

*In their lives they (men) started off under mum. Mums doing everything for them. Mum telling them stop that. So women have always been too strong for them (men). And then they get into marriage, they have a wife, women are very strong in marriages. In my own culture where I come from, the Samanyikas', the women vanototonga, muri mumusha chaimo hapana zvirango zvinoitwa anamai vedu vasipo, (Women are in powerful positions in the family in the Manyika tribe and there is nothing that is done if our mothers are not there) so again, for man, politics is something. They want to keep the political space to themselves.*

Mutsvangwa explains further.
*They look at women and they see that they are too strong and they come again to the political ground, then they (men) really don't have any space anymore but look it's about educating men. It's about educating them. Let's take the fears out of them that once the woman is around me she is going to act like a mum to me, because as women it's natural we micro. I don't want to call it micromanage but as women we go into detail.*

Monica Mutsvangwa is one of the young women who left the country to join the liberation struggle in the 1970's.

Monica Mutsvangwa has held a number of posts in the ZANU PF party and the government. She is currently the Minister of Women's Affairs, Community, Small and Medium Enterprises.

Some of her responsibilities in parliament have been; she was part of the 25 select Committee Members who were spearheading COPAC, and she was the co-Vice Chair. She was the Chairperson of the portfolio committee on indigenization and empowerment which entailed a lot of work. A delegate of the SADC Parliamentary forum were she was Treasurer for the Executive for 2 years. She is also a technical advisor when it comes to reading bills to members of her party ZANU PF.

Mutsvangwa encourages women to be active in

politics than to criticize from an aloof postion. *I feel we need to really get away from the idea of sitting back and reading and watching news and going on internet and then critisice. We need to do something as Zimbabweans and especially when we talk of women. We can never attain the 50/50 if women do not get out of that home and say look I need to participate in politics. We need women to get out there. It is so sad for a country which has had so many good policies about education to install few highly educated women in Parliament.*

It seems educating women is not being involved in mainstream politics and Mutsvangwa feels this is letting down a lot of women. *It makes me so angry and I always say to myself to be an MP, it entails representing people but at the same time it is just not about picking somebody who represent people who will not be able to understand a bill, to read a bill and understand it or to say okay where exactly is our country and where does it want to go because there are 3 things which a parliamentarian has to do. Representative, okay, you have to talk to your people in the same language, bring their issues to Parliament and take back issues from Parliament to them but there is another important one, it's a Legislative Body, Parliament. It's about understanding bills when the Executive brings up new Acts, one has to read and understand that language for you to participate, to contribute something which is useful, otherwise this is the biggest problem that we have and that should be our next step forward.*

There are a number of challenges which women face as they try to chat their way into mainstream politics. The biggest challenge is that of confidence.

*So I think we need the right women at the right place. So I think it's a question of being confident of yourself. Once you are confident of yourself and say I can do it, even if you walk into that room full of men, if they try to make jokes about you, if you ignore it and continue and have your goals achieved, they will end up respecting you.*

# Women in Parliament

Acceptability issues: if you want to be accepted then maybe you will never be a politician, you just can't expect to walk in a room full of men and expect them even before you open your mouth to accept you. You get into that room and speak your mind and what you know and they will respect you.

If you are yourself and you are capable, then they feel threatened and *this will only go away when there are more women at the top, because then men will see that no, no, no, the women are just as good as them. And they are here to do the job so that we achieve the result. We are getting there, the good thing is education, the system and the policies of this country have also promoted the girl child and this is the thing which we should be very proud of because we have a lot of women who are very educated and professional and experts in different walks of life. And if we can as women start celebrating each other and making sure that what the other woman has done should be celebrated and should be passed down to the girl child because we are their idols.*

In Zimbabwe women continue to fight to be in mainstream politics. Sarudzayi Chifamba–Barnes a Gender and Political Activist encourages more education, a free and fair campaigning arena as well as introducing a gender quota system for the selection of parliamentarians in the constitution which could help increase women involvement in politics. Countries where quotas for women have been written into the constitution or introduced through national legislation include Rwanda, Uganda, Argentina where it is mandatory that 30 per cent of elective posts be reserved for women, and India where 33 percent of the seats in local municipal bodies are reserved for women. Rwanda is the first country in the world with female majority in parliament, with 61.25% in the lower or single house and 38.46% in

**Tatenda Mavetera**

**Fadzai Mahere**

**Sandra Ndebele**

**Elisabeth Valerio**

the Senate, surpassing the 30 percent set aside for women. New Zealand and Sweden ¬are among the countries with the highest political representation of women in the world. New Zealand has 50.42% of women in the lower or single house and Sweden has 46.99% of women in the lower or single house. It is arguable that women can change policy agenda, as they can lobby for higher priority to social policy issues like education, health and pensions as opposed to higher budgets for defense. While women in Zimbabwe have high dreams to reach the 50/50 mark it seems a pipe dream because they are still far away from the quota system that other countries have achieved.

Women in Zimbabwe have tried to get into politics through the women's wings in their political parties, (Women's League – Zanu PF (The Zimbabwe African National Union – Patriotic Front) and Women's Assembly – MDC (The Movement for Democratic Change) and CCC (The Citizens Coalition for Change). Unfortunately, it seems most women become too comfortable in the women's league and fail to penetrate the main structures. *While the women's wing is good for development, Eunice Sandi a veteran politician encourages women that it should not keep them away from the male domain especially during elections. You are there, you are fixed up, at a corner somewhere doing your own thing as women, and you don't see the other side. You don't even want to, that's why we are still challenging each other so much and because of that we are not getting there. I believe we should focus with the agenda of promoting women in the manner that it should be, the manner is don't challenge a woman who is already in a position, get the positions that the men are holding so that you become more in the set-up. What is the point of having 10 women out of 160 men? It does not work! Then you go there and you fight for those 10 posts.*

**Eunice Sandi Moyo**

Her sentiments were echoed by **Lucia Matibenga** who has spent most of her time fighting for women's rights. Her activism started in the labour movement, she was the Minister of Public Service in the GNU government 2009 - 2013.

*I can tell you that in politics things are still difficult for us women, because of the women's wings groups. It is as if we should be fighting from our corner as women, we seem to be conditioned to fight for mafufu (crumbs). What we should do as women is to use the women's wings in our parties as factories to push women in the main wing. We should make sure that once we have a woman in the main wing we do everything in our power to have her stay there. You see, and the women are beginning to talk about that in the women's caucus of Parliament for example, but I am also saying that the women themselves need to interrogate their own organizations and say women's league, what role do we want it to play in the party? Is it just auxiliary? Are we going to the main? Or also in the main of playing main politics and how are we going to do that?*

*Because parties like the ANC, Zanu PF, and ZAPU, have had women's wings since 1963 but those names we used to hear when we were young in the women's league have not yet graduated to be in the main. Do you mean that they are* **madhonofisi** *(a lock which is not removed from the door), which do not grow up, because I would want us to fix that. Whenever we have a women's wing congress we should make sure that we remove the whole top leadership and have it in the mainstream, and have new women. It is time to transform those women's assemblies of this world.*
She charged.

# WOMEN'S PARLIAMENTARY CAUCUS GROUP

# Women's Parliamentary Caucus Group

**A**Women's Caucus Group was formed bringing together women from different political parties to try and address the problem that women are facing as they try to chart their way into the political arena.

The aim of establishing a Women's Parliamentary Caucus was for women parliamentarians to rise above party politics and address issues of common concern as women.

The Zimbabwe Women's Parliamentary Caucus was launched in October 2001 in response to the SADC Parliamentary Forum initiative with the assistance of AWEPA - The Association of European Parliamentarians with Africa.

The operations of the Caucus are guided by a Constitution which provides for, among other things, membership and management of the Caucus

Membership to the Caucus is open to all Zimbabwean Women Members of Parliament and Associate Members, upon payment of a prescribed fee.

An Associate Member is any former woman Member of the Parliament of Zimbabwe.

However, Associate Members are not entitled to take part in the management of the Caucus and cannot vote.

The composition of the Management Committee in the 7th Parliament was as follows:

a) Chairperson - **Hon. B. Nyamupinga (ZANU PF)**
b) Vice Chairperson - **Hon. K. Chabuka (MDC-T)**
c) Secretary - **Hon. S. Ncube (MDC-T)**
d) Vice Secretary - **Hon. A. Ndhlovu (ZANU PF)**
e) Treasurer - **Hon. B. Chikava (ZANU PF)**
f) Committee Members – **Hon M. N. Mandaba (ZANU PF); Hon. A. Muloyi Sibanda (MDC-T);**
g) Ex-Officio Members - **Hon. O Muchena (ZANU PF), Hon. N.M. Khumalo (MDC), Hon. M. Matienga (MDC-T), Hon.**
h) **Patron of the Caucas – Hon. E. Madzongwe (ZANU PF)** (President of the Senate).
h) The Director Research, Mrs. Christine Mafoko, assisted by Ms. Farai Hondonga provided the administrative secretariat of the Caucus.

*Beater Nyamupinga (left) and Keresenzia Chabuka (right)*

Since its inception in 2001, the Caucus achieved some of the following in line with its objectives and Plan of Action, the; **Sexual Offences Bill, Constitution of Zimbabwe Amendment No. 17 Bill, Domestic Violence Bill and Gender Mainstreaming in Legislation Objectives**

It is not only in parliament that women are spearheading the political agenda for women's emancipation and the 50/50 representation in politics but across the board. It is only when women are in every structure of the society's decision making that they will be a feeder system to the main political structures from grassroots to –parliament. Since the 1980's when Zimbabwe attained independence women have held posts as permanent secretaries, ambassadors, etc.

**Angeline Makwavarara** was the first woman permanent secretary and she was also the first female ambassador at independence. Makwavarara also opened those closed doors in other fields; she was the first print journalist and the first black Nursing Tutor.

Some of the women who have followed in her footsteps as ambassadors are; **Amina Hughes** who was ambassaodor in Sweden, **Trudy Stevenson** (late) was ambassador to Senegal, **Chipo Zindoga** in Namibia, **Jacquiline Zwambila** ambassador to Australia, **Thandiwe Dumbutshena** in Malawi (late), **Gertrude Takawira** was Ambabssador to Zambia, **Rudo Chitiga** was Ambassador to France, **Charity Manyeruke** is Ambassador to Rwanda and **Hilda Suka Mafudze** in Sudan.

In the constitution making we also saw women taking influential positions amongst them were Oppah Muchinguri, Monica Mutsvangwa and Jessie Majome. It is through the constitution that women will decide how their lives are going to be run. Monica Mutsvangwa was part of the 25 select Committee Members who were spearheading COPAC, and she was the co-Vice Chair. It is through COPAC that she was pushing for equal representation of women in government.

The constitutional public arena is the most important arena for making advances and for changing, turning around and undoing this harm that the society has

**Angeline Makwavarara**

been doing to women. While it has been a challenge bringing to the fore issues of gender balance, Majome will not tire discussing issues to do with the emancipation of women and equal opportunities.

Majome wishes to see super structures corrected, and the laws that regulate our country in the constitution, if this is not done women will not realize the fruits of other wonderful things that they are doing across the board. She encourages women to demand equality. *So in the outreach you would find that women were the majority of participants in this exercise, at least physically they were present, they were there, their bodies were right there. They came out in their numbers and they outnumbered men and the good thing is that from those meetings there came out a very clear call for 50/50, it was clear women want equality in the constitution and what's left now is then for those demands to be reduced to writing so that we have constitutional guarantee of equality between men and women and an end to discrimination right through the constitution.*

Majome also sites economic challenges that women face as a drawback, as they fail to fund their campaigns and projects when elected. Whereas men are sounder economically and the fact that they are the Captains of Industry they have an advantage over women as they network easily with their male counterparts. While they are women who are also influential in industry they are not as many as man. *We need to start engaging in dialogue with women in industry so that they understand the need to do networks and also support women in politics because as a woman If I am going to be knocking on the doors of the Captains of Industry (who are men), I might not be understood, because unfortunately we have a long way to go also in having women's sexuality taken out of politics, because of sometimes how people relate to us.* Jessie Majome explained.

**Amina Hughes**

**Trudy Stevenson**

**Jaqueiline Zwambila**

**Gertrude Takawira**

**Thandiwe Dumbutshena**

**Rudo Chitiga**

While economic challenges have been cited as a drawback for women politicians particularly when they are campaining, Sithembiso Nyoni encourages women to use human and social capital in order to be able to campaign and be involved in politics. Nyoni advices women to look for resources around them, what they have in their midst and use that to help them when campaigning. *Make sure you have the resources. Do you have a car? If you don't have, make sure you have human resources, the social habitants, either have capital or social capital, people will help you. She goes on to explain social capital. I have social capital as well and my biggest social capital is my family, I have a good husband, I have good children, I have a good family who understand me, who support me, that is very important.* That is the social capital that Sthembiso Nyoni is talking about, people around a woman politician – family and the community can be of great help when campaigning.

**Sthembiso Nyoni** *(top)* **Jessie Majome** *(bottom)*

# WOMEN LEARNING FROM THEIR EXPERIENCES ...

# Women Learning from their Experiences – Not giving up

**W**hat have women learnt from their Experiences? Are women politicians also helping other women to climb up the ladder? With all the experiences they have gone through are women in high positions in the political arena helping and supporting other women to rise to higher levels of politics and also encouraging and holding the hands of those women to climb the political ladder to be in the political realm. Eunice Nomthandazo Sandi Moyo who has been in politics for almost six centuries, shares her observations.

**Eunice Nomthandazo Sandi Moyo**

*If you look at the slaves who work at plantations and the slave who work in the house (do you understand me?) the slave who works in the house thinks they are better and can never defend your rights because you will disturb it in their comfort zone. So the truth is women have nobody who stand for them as women. It does not matter where they are as long as they are part of the government, they do not see the need for them to check on another woman. They are afraid of being fired because they are slaves just like you who are not there. They are scared that they will be fired if they talk about you.*

**Joyce** - What do you mean if she talks about you?

*That you need to be freed, to be a free woman. They are comfortable but they are scared to help another woman. We tried to put Teurai (Joice Mujuru), we tried our best and she was in (as vice president) and they used us (women) to destroy her because of the same thing I have told you, that the one inside is afraid to challenge anything because she is comfortable.*

**Margaret Dongo also adds her voice.**
You know always women want to reinvent the wheel. At every stage everyone else feels as a pioneer. We don't have this continuation were people would want to emulate from what the previous team has done – the Margaret Dongo's, the Mavis Chidzon-

ga's, the Mrs. Tungamirayi. To say how did they ferry during their time. Why don't we take up from there? You know the problem with women is that they will have to reinvent their own thing because they don't have this continuation and want to believe that, one way or the other we have to force it. We have to create it. Have a look the reason why we have male counterparts staying longer in parliament it is because they have these experiences that they share

and in fact they accept that. For women they always feel that the moment we get a position, we have this Queen Bee Syndrom you know – I am big and cannot communicate with somebody because I am there. I think women need to learn and open up and say this is a process, tomorrow I will drop it somebody should pick it from here and continue. So I want to believe that in future the women parliamentarians that are there should actually benefit from the women parliamentarians who were there. They can take it up. It's true we had our weaknesses, but one thing they should also realise is that we had our strength and then what they need to do is now to build on our strength and to build on our weakness as well.

Thokozani Kuphe supports Margaret Dongo's views. She encourages women to learn from their mistakes.

**Thokozani Khupe**

*Let us learn from our mistakes and use those mistakes as a stepping stone to success. Let us admit as women that we have made mistakes. Yes we have made mistakes because we constitute 52% of our population.*

*There is no ways we can continue crying, screaming and shouting to say; 'no we are not being represented equally. No we are being short changed'. Ladies let's do away with this victim mentality, let's do away with this cry baby mentality. Let's stand up on our two feet. Let's start fighting for ourselves. We can make it.*

# The Importance of Women Being in the Political Space

**Betty Mtero**

It is important that women be part of the political space as this creates a gender balance society and also women feel that they belong as full citizens. This also give women confidence and pride and self-actualization. This enhances and promotes normalization and the culture of celebrating women as leaders in the political sphere.

## BETTY MTERO

Betty Mtero feels that after independence many women were diverted from participating in active politics because of the excitement which was brought by the independence. *Now they have realized that there is no one who can articulate their problems for them in parliament except themselves.* Although women are fighting to have a bigger representation in parliament, people still need a lot of civic education to realise how important it is to have women in parliament. Betty Mtero feels today's campaign has become too complicated and expensive, which is a stumbling block for many women.

## ANGELINE MASUKU

*As I see it now when we talk about parliament where decisions are made about the running of the country. I think we are not going forward. I am not happy. What I can say is that let us learn that if a woman has a talent/gift, it is for all the women. That gift or talent will not just uplift only her but is for all the women. Let us help each other and be there for each other, especially with the young ones. I am always telling them that you young people stand up and be counted. My generation did their work, and it is there for all to see. We brought independence. Now it's time for you to do your work, especially to be part of the governing of this country, be there were issues to do with the country are mapped out. Young women must be part of governance*

**Angeline Masuku**

**Beater Nyamupinga**

## BEATER NYAMUPINGA

*Because for me I feel that the country is committing suicide by having a 52% just put aside and taking 1% into leadership where is the 51%, we want to see it participating. Not only in Parliament but also in all the decision-making positions, we want to be there. That's why when indigenization comes or economic empowerment is coming out we are missing out because our women are not positioned in strategic places. Hence we remain poor and when we are poor, elections have been commercialized, we will lose them but if we are economically empowered we will achieve because it is easy when you have resources.*

*I was saying that if we are not economically empowered it's very difficult to achieve the 50/50. I know in this house very few people would not want to come to Parliament, but how can we all can come there, with those strategies we must have them in place*

## MAINA MANDAVA

Maina Mandava - *We have a lot of knowledge even those women you look down upon, they understand all this. Education is just to perfect their understanding so that things can go accordingly but women we can do it. I think women have realised that they should be in positions of authority because during COPAC (The Constitution Parliamentary Select Committee) – Women demanded 50/50 up to chieftainship which means that women are realising that we need to wake up so that we get into all structures/places of authority.*

**Emelda Maina Mandava**

Joyce: The number of women is dropping since 2000. What is the problem?

*You know what it is about our attitude. It is something that we need to deal with but if we continue talking about it, it will be alright.*

**Joyce** - attitude of Women or men?

*Amongst ourselves as women but it will be corrected if continue to talk about it.*

A veteran politician Emelda Maina Mandava feels politics is also for women's self-actualization. *I encourage women to be involved in politics. It helps women in general and the woman politician herself. As a woman politician you become knowledgeable about a lot of things, your horizons broaden by being in politics. I would like to give as an example that it is because of*

*being a politician that is why I am in COPAC, which will help me as a person and also to help others. It helps me with my confidence, dignity and when you see me, "Handiti munoti Senator vasvika, ehe zvinondipawo self actualization (When you see me you say the Senetor is here, it gives me self actualization).*

## AGNES DETE

*For a woman to be in politics, in decision making is that whatever is decided for the country's budget development, women should also be there because that is where we end up seeing issues of women lagging behind. For instance, the budget favours men more than women. I can give an example - issues of maternity,*

**Agnes Dete**

you find that there are women who die in the materni-ty which means it will not be properly resourced. So if a woman is part of governance/politics she will know that another woman has no water, they need to have a borehole. A woman needs medicines, they need linen, and you need everything so that a woman can be com-fortable and well. So we say in all these places a woman should have a representative. Wherever decisions are made, women should be there because as women we are few. If we were many we could see change but now we are few because if the number of men is more than that of women it means that even if we add our voice we are few. What I would like to advice is training to women. Women should be trained and should be given resources. Any development must go to women.

## PATRICIA NDLOVU

*Patricia Ndlovu*

I would encourage women that were there is a good thing people will say what they want (bad things). You will be intimidated in order to instill fear in you but that should not make you give up. Our goal as women is not that we want to control men. No. We want to be in pol-itics so that we work together with men and build our country Zimbabwe so that we can all be happy.

So I am saying let us help each other, by putting our heads together with men so that we can register prog-ress and things can go the way they are supposed to. I want to encourage other women who are still afraid that there is nothing to fear, we will still remain the wives of our husbands but when we go to our councils (as councilors) we will introduce policies that will im-prove the life of a woman.

Patricia Ndlovu who was the only woman councilor in Beitbridge in 2011 feels it is important for a woman to be in politics - *Everything that we do is politics, even if we may choose not to believe it. Wherever you walk its politics! The water that you drink is politics!* Said Pa-tricia Ndlovu, as she explained why it is important for women to be in politics as councilors and parliamen-tarians. She would like to encourage men to support their wives to be in politics. As women politicians are working towards 50/50 representation in parliament. She advises men not to be scared that women want to be in the highest decision making body in the country – politics.

*We encourage fathers (our husbands) to give us sup-port we cannot be alone in this we need men to also support us. We have been advocating for women's rep-resentation in parliament as a lone voice. Isn't it nice to be called the husband of the President or Minister? It is something to be proud of to know that your wife is one of the people bringing development to the city, which can only happen when a woman is into active politics.*

## THOKOZANI KHUPE

*Women are serious organisers. They organise in their homes, their work places, they organise in politics. When it comes to elections you will hear our political leadership saying women the time has come start running around. Women will then stand up and run around organising people. They will do door to door campaigns. When it comes to the day of voting who votes it is women. Look at the queues, they are dominated by women. The women are the ones who elect leaders in their positions. This is who we are. We do all that. But, the problem comes when the leadership is about to elect cabinet ministers. Will hear them talking about 'Oh no we want women of quality.' That is what they want. But as women were doing door to door campaigns did anyone ask for quality? Ladies this is a serious case. If you look at the women, look at their energy that they have. Look at the brain power that women have. Anyone to say oh we want women of capacity. Capacity is the ability of doing something.*

*The fact that we organise people to go and vote that is capacity on its own. But what men forget again is that when they talk about capacity they forget that those same women who are said not to be of capacity are the ones who made those men who are not of capacity to be of capacity at the end of the day. There is no one who started by doing grade 7 without doing grade 1.*

*We learn in the process. We grow in the process and this must be acknowledged. That is where women are eliminated because we end up not being in that cabinet, you end up not seeing the door of that parliament, but I said earlier that, that's were policies are formulated. That's were laws are made. That's were budgets are passed. Where are you when all these things happen? That's when we start crying about there is no equality ha? Because we have been eliminated!!!!* She charged!

## RUTH CHINAMANO

**Joyce** - What is your message to women?

*My message to women is that women lets work together. Let's understand each other. Let us teach each other. Even in homes. Even in a one room home. You teach your mother ABCD. One plus one. She must know simple arithmetic. She must know simple English. So*

*Thokozani Khupe*

*Ruth Chinamano*

**(From left to right) Virginia Muchenje, Agnes Dete, Virginia Katyamaenza, Alice Chimbudzi**

*that she knows her rights. That woman will not vote for someone who she has not seen in her life, be it a man or a woman. She will vote for someone who is not only going to be happy with her during the election, after the election forget her and be in surbubs not knowing what she is eating. Not knowing when she is sick. At least if she votes for someone who is responsible and voting must be on merit not taking anyone who is just going to sit in parliament but people who are going to speak about the problems of their people in parliament.*

Now that women know better, we hope they will vote other women into parliament and support each other.

It is important to have women in key positions, in the forefront, in the running of the country. If women are in decision making, it will benefit other women, as they have the opportunity to actually shape and influence decisions on how the country is run.

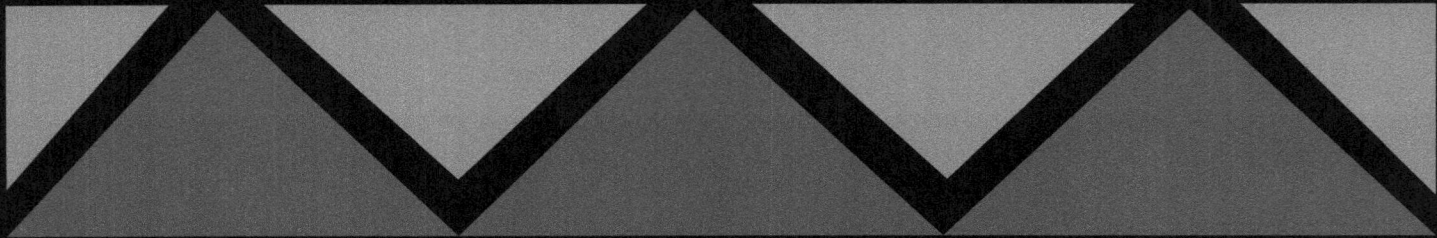

# WOMEN POLITICIANS/ PARLIMENTARIANS OF THE 7TH PARLIAMENT PROFILES

# SHORT STORIES OF WOMEN POLITICIANS -
# Women Politicians/ Parliamentarians of the 7th Parliament Profiles

**Bhudha Masara Sibusisiwe (MDC –T) 2011**

**Sibusisiwe Bhudha** was born in 1971 in Kwekwe. She became involved in politics in 1999 first as a member of the National Constitutional Assembly. She believes in participation to effect change in governance. She says that she realized when she campaigned for the MDC, they were campaigning for men. *"We thank organizations like WIPSU and the Women's Trust which has opened our minds as women, we are well informed."*

The road to politics has been rough for her because of male domination and violence. In 2005 Matabeleland north failed to get a female MP, "we could not do it as women because of economic power" she says. *"We continued to campaign for men. In 2005 the party split, I was still in the National Assembly and the leader was allowed to be in the main body but most decisions were led by men. Women could not move motions...".*

About achieving 50/50 representation, she believes that it must start must start at the lowest level. *"In 2009 I was promised governorship but some of our big people were not happy and I was not sworn in."*

Women in her party seemed not to be worried that she was not sworn in. She concludes by saying that women should rise above party politics and consider seriously how to achieve out 50/50 representation. Sibusisiwe does not believe in riding on men's backs for recognition.

**Bhuka Flora (ZANU PF** - *Minister of State for Special Affairs Responsible for Lands, Land Reform and Resettlement since 2005- MP Gokwe / Nembudziya)* *-2011*

**Flora** has a BA General Degree from the University of Zimbabwe, and worked as a school teacher from 1991 to Mid-1995 when she became a head-teacher at Svibe Secondary School. In 1999, she was appointed Constitutional Commissioner during the Constitutional Commission, and in 2000 she was appointed Minister of State in the Office of the Vice President Responsible for Land Reform Programme.

She was the Chairperson of the Zimbabwe Women's Parliamentary Caucus and an Executive Member of the SADC Regional Women's Caucuses from 2004 to 2009

**Chabuka Keresenzia (MDC –T)** - *Deputy Chairwoman of the Women Parliamentarian Caucus – Senator for Mutare)* - *2011*

**Keresenzia** joined the MDC in 1999, and helped to set up MDC structures in Mutare. She was elected ward Chairwoman before she became Chairwoman for Manicaland Province and a Senator. She wants 50% representation for women in parliament, and encourages middle class women to engage in politics as everyone is affected by political decisions.

The civil society needs to educate people at grassroots level on the benefits of equal representation. She was happy that women occupied the positions of Vice President and Deputy Prime Minister (2011). She sees the 'pull-her-down syndrome' from fellow women as an obstacle to women empowerment. She encourages the media to fully play the role of covering women projects.

She enjoys the support of her husband.

**Chaderopa Fungai (ZANU PF - MP Sanyati Constituency). - 2011**

**Chibhagu Gertrude (ZANU PF - Senator for Guruve-Mbire) - 2011**

**Fungai Chaderopa** was born in 1949 and grew up in Bulawayo before her family moved to Nembudziya (Sanyati). In 1980 she became Zanu Pf Chairwoman for Chenjiri for two years, and MP in 2008. Her husband is also a politician and very supportive.

She discourages MPs from engaging in partisan politics, which hinders development. The main hurdle for many aspiring female politicians is inter-party politics (de-campaigning each other), violence and men using beer (intoxicating youths) to campaign, which leads to violent campaigns. When she was MP for her constituency she bought roofing and painting for schools in her constituency, and wanted to repair the clinic at Chenjiri which was built by donors using boards that are now dilapidated. She wishes to have more women to be councillors, and when they leave their positions they should be replaced by women and not men. She advocates for better pay for civil servants and recognition of village health workers who work very hard. She wants more young people to join politics but to desist from violence.

**Gertrude Chibhagu** started political activism soon after independence. She worked for Mashonaland Central Province for 31 years, and was chosen by the people; men, women, and youths, to represent them as a Senator. She stood against four other women at Primaries, and won. She campaigned on foot, carrying a bottle of water (to quench thirst), and a packet of roasted dry maize *(maputi)*. The constituency was reserved for women to achieve gender balance. Gertrude believed she won because of her good working relationship with people of all backgrounds; rich and poor, in her area.

She initiated community development projects in the Lower Valley; building new schools, improving agriculture and introducing cash crops such as cotton. Because of her good work with people, she also won 1 706 from the Doma people (Bushmen) who generally do not want to see people from outside their community. She also upgraded women's lives, and had four female councillors in Upper Guruve. She believes that there should be more women in parliament and decision-making positions because they work hard for their constituencies.

Gertrude Chibhangu got support from her husband, who encouraged her projects. She said being in Parliament has been an eye-opener for her. It proves that anyone, especially women, can achieve anything. She was educated by her brother after her father refused to buy her books, and believed in educating boys. In Parliament she is confident to move any motion as long she was representing the wishes of her people.

**Chikava Betty (ZANU PF - MP for Mt Darwin East and Member for Central Committee)-2011**

The late **Betty Chikava (nee Ndoro)** started politics in 1960 in Highfields as a ZAPU youth activist and later joined ZANU under Ndabaningi Sithole in 1963. As a nurse she sourced food and medicine for freedom-fighters. She felt that women are still oppressed through gender roles which favour men and boys.

With little resources available, Chikava worked hard to develop her constituency. She sourced footballs for youths, linen for the hospital, books for schools, and various clothing through World Vision. Betty Chikava believed that through motivation and leadership workshops, women will become more involved in politics, and that for many women, joining politics becomes elusive because it involves vigorous campaigning and many days away from family.

She advocated for 50/50 gender representation at all leadership levels, and wanted more young women to engage in politics because most of the women in current leadership positions are getting older, so there is need to groom younger females.

**Chimbudzi Alice (Zanu-PF - Senator for Mount Darwin and Politburo Member)-2011**

**Chimbudzi Alice** has an interest in women and the girl child issues, and believes that emancipation of women comes through participation in decision making; hence women should attend meetings to air their grievances or get elected into local and central government positions

She started at cell level as chairwoman until she became a member of the Central Committee, Politburo and Senator in 2005. After attending the Beijing Women's Conference in 1995, she was inspired to launch the Girl-Child Program and mobilized female councilors and female teachers to sponsor two girls each from a primary school of their choice. Some of the girls later assumed leadership roles in teaching, police, and agriculture. She was chosen by people to represent her constituency as a senator. She was instrumental in increasing the number of female councillors to 14 seats out of 35 wards, the highest female representation at local government level in the rural areas.

Chimbudzi believes that all leaders should thrive to improve the well-being of the people they lead, and leads by example, for example, she ploughs the land for people in need in her Ward using her tractor; and that it is good to know how people you lead make a living.

**Chinomona Mabel (ZANU PF - Former Deputy Minister Home Affairs and MP for Mutoko)-2011**

**Mabel Chinomona** (nom de guerre Memory Matimaitei) joined the liberation struggle in 1975 at the age of 15. She is a survivor of the Chimoio massacre.

After the war she trained as a secretary and became an MP for Mutoko in 1990. At primaries she faced resistance from traditional leaders who did not want a woman MP. In 1997 she became Deputy Minister for Home Affairs. Chinomona was instrumental in changing women police uniforms to include trousers, and going to Freedom Camp (Zambia) and Chimoio to rebury the war victims. She feels that leaders who start from grassroots level (bottom-up) understand people's issues and appeal to people.

Mabel Chinomona worked with Plan International to provide fencing for schools and building classroom blocks and toilets. She is using her allocation of money from the Constituency Development Fund to provide roofing for schools, providing grinding mills and generators in different wards. She is also assisting youth's groups and women to start a poultry project, providing pre-schools, toilets and electricity for clinics and painting schools and repairing some boreholes.

Mabel believes that women MPs should be role models and lead by example. She feels that for many women leaders, if their partners/husbands are not supportive, the marriage can either end (divorce), or the woman can quit politics. She also wants women leaders to groom young people to take over, and for MPs to rise above partisan politics and stop heckling each other in Parliament at the expense of development. Leaders should appreciate diversity and different ideologies. She is currently President of Senate.

### Chitsa Enna (MDC-T – Senator for Masotsha Ndlovu) - 2011

The late **Chitsa** started politics at a very young age when she joined ZAPU, but decided to leave politics when Zanu and Zapu forged a unity accord. She re-

joined politics through the Trade Union, and was instrumental in the formation of the MDC. She realized that it would be very difficult for women to become MPs, because, "Men made sure that they did not give us a chance, they made it impossible for women to be MPs." She decided to work for the party in a different capacity; as the National Vice President of the Women's Assembly, and in 2008 she was elected as Senator. "When one is elected as an MP in an area, you are not just elected for your party but for the whole nation." It is this attitude that saw Chitsa working well with her constituency as a Senator.

Enna Chitsa had two MPs in her constituency. She would meet with them and they took their discussions to the Lower House. She believed that women should be in politics because they are natural leaders although they are suppressed by society. Enna believed that political violence is not good for women, as it deters them from becoming involved. On 50/50 representation she believed it should be enforced by law. Although some husbands do not support their wives, Enna got support from her late husband, family and members of her church.

### Dr Chung Fay (Former Deputy Minister of Administration for the Ministry of Education, and Minister of Education) - 2011

**Fay** was born in 1942 to parents of Chinese heritage. Her grandparents came from the Canton Province of China in 1904. In Rhodesia even the Chinese children were segregated against at school "unless your parents were wealthy enough to send you overseas, or to South Africa, you couldn't enjoy primary and secondary education." she said in an interview with Ruth Weiss. Her aunt remained in the same class for five years because her parents were told "We don't allow any Chinese in this school." Going to school with Coloureds politicized Fay, because they were a rejected people by both the Africans and the Whites.

She found the colonial education for African children deplorable, and a symbol of oppression itself which only allowed one in five children to access secondary education. In 1973 Fay joined ZANU during the liberation struggles but was forced to exile in Tanzania and Mozambique. In 1980 she served as Deputy Minister of Administration for the Ministry of Education, and Minister of Education in 1988. Fay remains an active advocate for women's education, leadership and empowerment efforts in Africa. She also co-founded the Forum for African Women Educationalists (FAWE), Women's University in Africa and Association for Strengthening Higher Education for Women in Africa (ASHEWA).

## Dete Agnes (ZANU PF – Senator for Mazowe) - 2011

**Agnes Angelina Dete** had 4 MPs under her constituency 2011. She supports the proposal for 50/50 representation, which she thinks will encourage female engagement in politics and decision making. 50/50 reflecting a zebra pattern, and will be beneficial to women especially as they will lobby for resources that benefit women, such as healthcare, maternity, water and sanitation, and that many women are dying needlessly in childbirth.

Dete started politics in 1962 and supported the liberation struggle by providing food and clothes to freedom fighters. She was inspired to join politics by the oppression that black people especially women experienced under white minority rule. Women were not allowed to own bank accounts or apply for ID cards.

Because of her history of working with women, they asked her to run for senate. Agnes was born in 1944 in Goromonzi where her parents worked on a farm.

Agnes Dete believes that many young women should be encouraged to join politics if they are educated on how it will benefit them and other women in general.

## Dongo Margaret (Former MP of Harare East) - 2011

**Margaret (Mtetwa) Dongo** was born in 1960, and joined the liberation struggle in Mozambique in 1975 where she was known as *Tichaona Muhondo* (nom-de-guerre). She is one of the survivors of the Chimoio massacres by the Rhodesian Security Forces. After independence she resumed her education (which she had aborted during the war); and later worked for Zimbabwe News Agency before becoming an MP for Harare East in 1990, she enlightened many woman in her constituency on political issues and encouraged and helped them to be economically independent. Margaret was instrumental for the formation of the Zimbabwe War Veterans Association in 1989 to campaign for the cause of war veterans who were destitute.

Margaret believes in gender empowerment and challenges all forms of gender oppression. She was the first female, to launch an opposition party, the Zimbabwe Union for Democrats, which is argued to have paved way for other opposition parties in the country. She believes in transparency, democracy and openness, and as an MP she was voted the parliament's most accessible member with a whopping 95 percent approval rating by the *Mirror magazine*.

In 2010 she won a Supreme ruling against a law which did not permit women to sign passport applications for their children. Only men were allowed to do so. Margaret does not believe in ministries of women's affairs to deal with women's issues, because *"women have problems in education, problems in finance, problems in all sectors so why should they say, 'Go to your own ministry! Fight your own battles and win?' This is divide and rule. This is what makes me take the position that I take because women suffered just the same as men in the camps and in the war".*

## Dube – Gombami Gladys (MDC-T - Senator for Mabutweni Constituency) - 2011

While most agree that women emancipation has been affected mostly by the way our society is structured under patriarchy. The late Gladys Dube felt that women themselves are not helping the situation and fuelling it by not working together to challenge gender disparities. *"When a woman is appointed to a position, she makes sure that she stays alone at the top and makes it impossible for other women to come there, maybe it is the way women were brought up that they want 'ukubukwa,' they want all men to look and admire them and that way they feel complete and if another woman comes along the attention will be divided."* She advises women to stop the mentality of thinking that they are flowers and have to be picked amongst all the other flowers.

Gladys Dube believed when addressing political issues with men, women need not to be confrontational. It does not help the situation at all. She encouraged women to engage men and to educate them. *"When someone is confronted they build ammunition and it does not help our situation as women. Again it*

*is those women who already are at the top who cause this confusion so that they stay alone at the top."*

At 47 year old Gombami, a mother of five children, wanted to find ways and work out strategies that can see women achieve 50/50 equal representation in Parliament. She believed that women should not remove ladders for other women when climbing the stairs, and should remember those women who have held the ladder for them to go up. *"We can sing 50/50 as much as we want but if we do not change our thinking it will remain just a song,"* she said. Dube a mother of five died at the age of 47.

## Professor Gaidzanwa Rudo (Associate Professor of Sociology at the University of Zimbabwe) - 2011

She ran as an independent candidate in the March 2008 election, and lost, but it was brave of her to run as an independent as a woman. She served as a Constitution Commissioner (1999-2000), and is on various boards and committees, including being a founder and trustee of the Women's University in Africa. She teaches Social Policy and is a feminist human rights activist and a mother. Professor Gaidzanwa believes in women empowerment through education, and criticized the 2012 financial budget as it would do nothing to improve education for females.

*"A salary-focused budget is not sustainable and that means there is not money for real education in 2012",* said Gaidzanwa.

She also argues that although the $30 000 allocation towards gender mainstreaming for tertiary education is a welcome development in the 2012 budget, it does not match with the extent of gender imbalances existing in tertiary education, and that "Funding schemes should be structured with the purpose of strengthening female participation in technical and scientific sector higher education," she said.

Women like Professor Gaidzanwa are needed in parliament as they discuss real issues affecting women.

## Goto Rosemary (ZANU PF – MP Hwedza South Constituency) - 2011

**Rosemary Goto,** born in 1946, comes from Hwedza, Mashonaland East Province. She started politics during the war. She was a Senator for Chikomba-Hwedza (2005-2008), and became MP for Hwedza South.

Goto sees lack of unity among women as the main obstacle to involvement in politics and decision making, and supports the positive role of WIPSU and NGOs in encouraging women participation through workshops. She supports the proposal for 50/50 representation and encourages women to support each other.

To challenge ageism Rosemary started an Athletics Tournament for people between the ages of 39 and 90 in her constituency which promotes physical health through sport, and both men and women participate. To support women in her constituency,

Rosemary bought some grinding mills for different communities because women were travelling for long distances to grind their corn. She believes in projects that support sustainable development such as gardening and farming.

She would want to see more women going for cultural exchange programmes to learn how other women are doing it. She herself went to Rwanda.

### Holland Sekai (Minister of State for National Healing, Reconciliation and Integration in the office of Prime Minister 2009 -2013) – 2011

**Sekai Holland** is a founding member of the Movement for Democratic Change and has spent much of her time in Australia, and married an Australian husband.

Sekai's political activism began in the 1960s, when, together with her spouse Jim Holland, they formed

Australia's Anti-Apartheid Movement and campaigned for Aboriginal rights. From 1973 to 1976 she was the Chairperson for Imurenga General Council of Zanu (Pacific and Asia, Australia and New Zealand). Hon Holland is a gender activist as well as political activist. She was also one of the founding members of the Zimbabwe Institute of mass Communication (ZIMCO). Holland was the MDC T Senator for Chizhanje, Harare province.

She was the MDC-T Minister of State for National Healing, Reconciliation and Integration in the office of Prime Minister (2009 -2013).

### Karenyi Lynette –Kore (MDC – T - MP Chimanimani West 2008-2013) - 2011

Elected MP for Chimanimani West in 2008, **Lynnette Karenyi** admits that it was not easy for her as a female politician from the oposition. She joined the

MDC in 1999, and was elected councilor for Chikanga Phase 2 Ward 16, Mutare, in 2003. The council was suspended in 2005. In 2006 she became the Provincial Secretary for Manicaland Province, and national organizing secretary for women. She feels that challenges faced by female politicians include inadequate resources to run successful campaigns, labeling, internal and inter-party violence.

She wants the government to reserve more constituencies for female parliamentarians to encourage women participation in politics, and feels that women are more empathetic to the needs of marginalized people.

Karenyi – Kore is currently Vice President for CCC (Triple C Party)

**Katsande Aqilina ( ZANU PF – MP Mudzi West) - 2011**

She was a mother of five, farmer, widow, and a politician! **Aqilina Katsande** believed that women are marginalized from occupying key decision-making positions in politics, yet women engage in community development projects that benefit women and children, and the few women who engage in politics get labelled as prostitutes or witches. She argues.

Born in 1960, Aqilina was elected MP for Mudzi East in 2005, beating her opponents with more than 8000 votes. She was also the Provincial Secretary for Women's League. As a female ward councilor and an MP, her major challenge were to fight cultural practices that oppress women and girls, such as marrying girl-children for food, or appeasing avenging spirits with virgin girls, both practices which were rife in her area.

**Katyamaenza Virginia (ZANU PF - Senator for Makonde) -2011**

Mother of 6, **Virginia Katyamaenza** is the Senator for Makonde, which incorporates Chinhoyi, Mhangura and Makonde Constituencies. She started politics at a young age, and was elected deputy head girl in Standard 6. Although she was bright at school, her dream to train as a nurse was thwarted because her parents did not believe in educating girl children. She married a politician, who later participated at the Lancaster House Conference. Virginia became a Chairwoman for a People's Movement in 1979; and Chairwoman for Chinhoyi District (1979-1984), and provincial Chairwoman in 1984. She was a member of the Central Committee.

Being a senator boosted her confidence, and she wanted more women to participate in politics and fight gender discrimination.

### Khumalo Tabitha (MDC – T – MP Bulawayo East) - 2011

**Tabita** was the Youth Chair for ZAPU and joined the liberation struggle in Zambia and came back in 1980. She joined the Cold Storage Company Worker's Union and later ZCTU. Because she was the only woman in the Union, she was often referred to as a prostitute.

She decided to join politics again because women

who make 52% of the population are still marginalized and underrepresented in decision making positions. "There are issues that literally affect women which won't affect men", and gives the lack of sanitary wear which can cause many infections to women as an example. From 1999 to 2005 she launched a campaign known as Dignity Period, and in 2005 she sourced 40 tonnes of sanitary towels from the Director of Asian Society in Africa.

The government needs to pay more attention to women's health, including making it easy for women to access free health screenings (Pap smear, mammography etc) because women are dying in large numbers from breast cancer and cervical cancer."

Tabitha does not believe in the pull-her-down syndrome, but that those men as the major decision-makers in women's lives control the way women operate, and stigmatize women who participate in workshops especially those carried out in hotels. Women can achieve 50/50 representation if they unite because *"As women we have the weapons of mass destruction, we are our own liberators, the onus is on us…"*

**Khupe Thokozani (Deputy Prime Minister; Vice-President of the Movement for Democratic Change-Tsvangirai, MP Makokoba 2009-2013) - 2011**

**Thokozani** was born in Bulawayo in 1963. She worked for the National Railways, and through trade union, later became Secretary for the Zimbabwe Congress of Trade Unions Women's Advisory Council in 1991. She joined the MDC through trade union, becoming its Secretary for Transport and Logistics, and Member of Parliament for Makokoba in 2000. In 2005 when the MDC split in two factions, she remained with the MDC led by Morgan Tsvangirai and became the Vice President of MDC-T. In 2009 she became the Deputy Prime Minister in the GNU government. In 2010 she led by example when she publicly declared that she had breast cancer, and shove her hair, which in a way raises breast cancer awareness and shows people that ministers are also human beings and prone to any illness.

The does not apologies for fighting for women's rights, at the re-launch of 50/50 representation she encouraged women not adopt the constitution if they are not well represented. She was Deputy Prime Minister for Zimbabwe and Vice-President of the Movement for Democratic Change-Tsvangirai, MP Makokoba 2009-2013.

**Mabhiza Gladys (ZANU PF - Central Committee Member, Senator for Seke Chikomba ) - 2011**

The late **Gladys Mabhiza** was born in 1957 in Seke Village, Gladys was a symbol of the challenges faced by the girl child in a patriarchal society. She was educated by her father up to Grade 7 only, but determined as she was to get an education, she later attended night school at Seke 3 to get a decent education. She later worked for a co-operative sewing uniforms, before becoming a security guard at Meikles Hotel and later worked at Greatermans shops for 18 years. She joined the Commercial Workers' Union and was instrumental in fighting for a pay rise of 45% for all Greatermans workers. She left her job in 2003 to become a full time politician. She was a member of Zanu Pf Central Committee and Senator for Seke Chikomba.

She empowered vulnerable women by giving them seeds such as Canoola to grow. Canoola is both a vegetable and an oil seed, and the women can squeeze the seeds to make vegetable oil. Seke, being devoid of natural vegetation, Gladys worked closely with EMA to encourage sustainable environmental management in her constituency. Gladys believed in empowering women to be self-reliant as a way of tackling poverty as she believed women know the issues that affect households. Gladys also believe that women need to be united and strategize when it comes to working with men, who can easily de-campaign women. "They know our power as women," she said.

## Madau Metrine (MDC – T - MP Beitbridge West) - 2011

**Metrine** was the first female Councilor in Beitbridge, and acknowledged that she joined politics after Mama Mohadi, who was the first female Senator, who encouraged women to be in politics. She chaired the Beitbridge Council before becoming an MP. Her place (as a councilor) was filled by another woman. Beitbridge then in 2011 had six female Councillors. "To be a good politician one has to go and meet others and learn what they do…the workshops by WIPSU have helped us that politics is not for men only," she said.

Metrine believes that she won both the primaries (against two women and the men) and against the MDC candidate because she had the support of women, who are no longer afraid of voting another woman. With the CDF money, she extended the clinic and built a house for nurses. She would have wanted to build a school so that children would not have to walk long distances to get to school. She gets support from her husband Major Madau, and does not feel intimidated to talk in parliament. "You don't go into politics because you have a degree, but because of the work that one does with the community, so there are certain things that I do not understand and he [husband]helps me."

Metrine married her husband in 1975, before he left to join the war but she waited for him. She wants Parliament to enact laws that punish rapists severely, including life behind bars. When a woman gets into parliament, it helps other women to get access to information, because women like to share [information].

**Madzongwe Edna (Senate President, Senator for Chegutu and Member of Zanu PF Politburo and Central Committee) - 2011**

**Edna Madzongwe** is the first woman since independence in 1980 to hold the position of Deputy Speaker of Parliament. She was born in 1943 and grew up in a family of politicians, many who participated in the liberation struggle, which brought about independence in 1980. Although a committed ZANU PF member, Madzongwe said her strength as Deputy Speaker was her impartiality in her interaction with all MPs when she was handling parliamentary business or officiating at parliamentary functions. Hon. Madzongwe is passionate about women's participation in politics and would like a situation where many women are actively involved in politics.

**Mahofa Shuvai (ZANU PF - Former MP for Gutu South) - 2011**

The late **Shuvai Mahofa** was appointed Deputy Minister of Youth, Gender and Employment Creation soon after the June 2000 parliamentary elections. She was a spirited and vociferous activist, Mahofa commanded senior and influential positions in ZANU PFs Politburo.

One of her goals she said, is to groom young women

to become top leaders in political office. She said her political vision was to see women empowered and taking part in decision-making processes in national politics, including the civil service, commerce and industry.

"Women suffer more when there is poverty and this is the situation in my constituency today. This is further aggravated by the fact that they are the ones responsible for the children, the sick and the elderly," She believed that women must be trained to join party politics from grass-root level so that they can compete at the same level with men. She said "Political parties are structured in such a way that is impossible for a woman to rise through ranks."

According to the *Standard Newspaper*, many people tried to dislodge her political career, but enjoyed the backing of some people within the party including the late Vice-President Simon Muzenda. She earned the title "The Iron Lady" of Zanu PF politics.

### Mahoka Sarah (ZANU PF - MP for Hurungwe East Constituency). - 2011

Born in 1966 in a family of politicians, **Sarah** joined politics to challenge the oppression of women. She supported the proposal for 50% female representation in parliament. "As natural nation builders, women are approachable, empathetic, and should occupy more powerful positions in governance.

Women bear the brunt of bad decisions made my male dominated institutions, and its more women than men who die in road accidents as they go out to look for resources. There should be a separate budget for women's projects. More needs to be done to change laws that oppress women, and gender violence is perpetuated by low court fines," she argues.

Sarah had three children and grandchildren, and got moral support from her husband.

**Majome Fungai Jessie (MDC-T MP for Harare West, Deputy Minister of Women's Affairs 2009-2013) - 2011**

A lawyer by profession, Jessie Majome was born in 1971. With her activism background, her understanding of the law, gender issues and her pursuit for justice, Majome's political career was destined for greater heights. However she has taken a break from active politics.

"I grew up in a politically charged environment, but I think the reason why I also got into it is because I had a kin sense of justice. I want all the time what is fair and what is just and you know I think it's just not right for anyone to do anything or hold down another person. I think it's the sense of justice that I've always have. I think that's the reason why I always speak out when things are unfair." From an early age, Jessie Majome has challenged most of society's structures in her quest for justice, including challenging gender

imbalances.

Majome encourages women to actively participate in the writing of the constitution no matter what political party they belong to. She believes that many women face financial drawbacks when it comes to funding their campaigns and projects when elected.

**Makone Theresa (Co-Minister Home Affairs, and MDC-T Chairperson of the National Assembly of Women, MP Harare North 2009-2013  - 20**

"I did not want to get into politics until my own life was affected economically. If I had the choice right now and the country was normal, I would rather be doing what I was doing and I was a successful business person," says **Theresa Makone** in an interview with Lance Guma (*Short Wave Radio Africa*). She says being the leader of women in the MDC is the highest privilege that she could ever attain, and is not doing it for herself but for women and Zimbabweans. In her interview with Guma, Theresa acknowledges thwarting her effort to work hard for the party, and "they spent a lot of money canvassing against me but you know what? The women told them to go to hell and I won resoundingly against their better judgment, so the people that matter to me are the women of Zimbabwe that I interact with, that I work with at the grassroots level who know where my heart is, who know my passion for the freedom of Zimbabwe."

## Mandaba Maina Imelda (ZANU PF – Senator for Masvingo) - 2011

**Imelda** became a Senator in 2008. To her it is very important to be involved in politics and decision making, especially since women understand issues that affect them and they can lobby for their enactment and implementation. Women are also patient when it comes to implementation and interpreting the laws to people. Laws regarding maternity leave and pay should not be decided by men but women

themselves. People need to change their attitude and appreciate women's potential as leaders. As a nurse Imelda contributed towards the construction of the Matrimonial Causes Act, and she was aware of her rights when she decided to divorce her husband. Because many women do not understand the Act, she believes that they suffer in marriages because they are not aware that they too can initiate divorce proceedings.

Imelda educated women on the proposal for the new constitution through COPAC. She is teaching women to start small businesses without borrowing loans, such as making candles and keeping bees for honey. Mandava urges all women to support each other, vote for each other because if they are divided, men take advantage.

## Mangami Dorothy (ZANU PF – MP Gokwe) - 2011

**Dorothy Mangami** started being active in politics in 1995. She was an MP for Zanu PF. Her main challenge was to balance the time between being with members of her constituency, Parliament and family.

She did not face major problems during her campaign apart from shortage of resources. *"I competed with a woman, my party decided that the position be reserved for a woman and only women competed in that constituency…it was not a tough thing as compared to when you are competing with a man with a lot of resources".* People applauded her because she consulted them; and in one area the people requested the construction of a footbridge, because during the rainy season it becomes difficult for people to cross the river to go to the shopping centre and school.

Mangami feels that women should create space for themselves because no one will create space for anyone.

**Manyeruke Jenia (ZANU PF - Secretary for Muzarabani, Senator for Mash Central Province 2008). - 2011**

**Jenia Manyeruke** was born in 1952, in Chikomba, her family moved to Muzarabani in 1966. She became the Political Commissar for ZANU in 1978, joined Women Action Group at independence and attended various leadership workshops, which heightened her gender awareness. Manyeruke became Senator in 2008, and did not face many challenges during primary elections because she had the support of women and youths.

Some women discouraged her from competing (out of fear), but she felt the need to challenge men and represent women. Although senators do not get financial help for projects, she makes follow-up when MPs in her constituency do some projects through CDF. She encourages more women to join politics because they will feel empowered and inspired. She wrote her O levels at the age of 58, and passed her driving license at the age of 54.

She believes that gender and age should not be seen as barriers from achieving anything. She wants WIPSU to carry out more workshops with women especially in rural and remote areas to encourage them to become active and get involved in decision making positions.

## Maposhere Dorcas (ZANU PF - MP Gokwe) - 2011

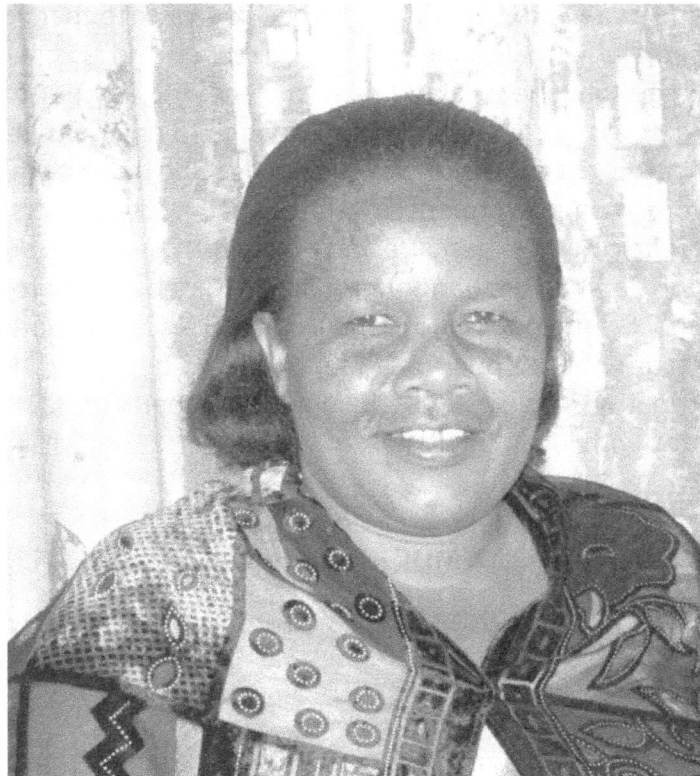

**Dorcas Maposhere** was born in 1960 in Chiredzi but her family moved to Gokwe. She was a collaborator during the war (chimbwido). She was chosen by 5 wards to represent them as MP.

As a female parliamentarian, she feels women at grassroots level feel free to talk to her about any issues affecting them, rather than talking to men. The challenge facing many women in parliament is confidence, but with regular workshops, Dorcas feels that her confidence is improving. She also feels that many women do not want to get involved in politics because of fear of being labelled; but that does not deter her, and she wants more women to get involved and promote each other.

She started youth tournaments and competition and winners got T-shirts. She is also working with women at ward level.

## Masaiti Evelyn (MDC – T - MP for Dzivarasekwa; MDC National Executive) - 2011

**Evelyn Masaiti**, nee Muzungu, was born in Bikita in 1965, and was an active ZANU PF supporter till 1999 when she joined the MDC and became MP for Mutasa constituency after a campaign marred by political violence in which her village and property were burnt to ashes. She also faced challenges at primary elections because of her tribe (Karanga) campaigning in Mutasa (Manyika).

In 2008 she was elected MP for Dzivarasekwa and Deputy Minister of Women Affairs, Gender and Community Development from 2009 till June 2010. She was in the MDC National Executive.

Evelyn urges all women to rise above party politics and work together, and feels that organizations like WIPSU and Women's Trust are making major contributions to help women become confident.

She believes that educating women is educating the nation while educating a man is educating an individual. She wanted Zimbabwe to fulfil the Gender protocol of 50/50 representation by 2015. Unfortunately we are now in 2023, and 50/50 has not been achieved. She feels that without proper implementation programme the Gender and Domestic Violence Act is ineffective, and she wants women to be uplifted socially, politically and economically.

**Angeline Masuku (Matabeleland South Provincial Governor & Politburo Secretary for Gender and Culture- ZANU PF - 2011)**

**Angeline Masuku** was born in 1936, and was appointed Governor and Resident Minister for Matabeleland South in November 2003, becoming the second woman after independence to hold such a post. She served as MP for Luveve constituency from 1990 to 1995, and is also the Secretary for the disabled in the ZANU (PF) Politburo. Masuku believed

that as a female Governor she had to work a lot harder than her male colleagues to be recognized, a challenge that she is taking by the horns. She vowed to work with the people in her Province to ensure that her term as Governor was successful. She believes in youths' empowerment since they are the fore bearers of the country's heritage and resources. Masuku supports animal husbandry projects in Matabeleland to boost cattle population, and irrigation since the food security of the people of Matabeleland depends on irrigation projects. Matabeleland is generally a dry area with low rainfall pattern.

**Matamisa Editor (MDC – T- Kadoma Central) - 2011**

**Editor Matamisa,** nee Tsomondo, who was the MDC MP for Kadoma, was born in Hwedza. She went to St Anne's Mission where the late Minister Mahachi was the school head-boy at the time. She was married in 1971, took care of her siblings after her father died, and trained as a teacher at Mkoba together with her husband, after she studied for O and Levels through correspondence.

She also studied for BA and Masters Degrees with Zimbabwe Open University. Because of her ability to challenge oppression, she was encouraged by her younger son to join politics, and represented the MDC in the 2000 mayoral elections.

She was elected the MDC Women's Coordinator in 2005 and MP in 2008.

**Matibenga Lucia (MDC-T MP for Kuwadzana, Governing Member of the International Labour Organisation- 2011)**

**Lucia Gladys Matibenga**, was Minister of Public Service in 2011-2013. She was born in Bulawayo and went to school at St Francis of Assisi in Chivhu. The late Josiah Tongogara was her husband's first cousin (not brother as some people believe). During the war she mobilized resources for freedom-fighters operating in Chirumanzu, Shurugwi, and Chivi. She married

one of the freedom-fighters who became one of the 12 MPs representing Zanu Pf in Midlands Province from 1980-1985. He died in 1990 and was buried at Gweru Provincial Heroes Acre.

She ceased to support Zanu Pf in 1986 after her husband was dropped from leadership position due to inter-party fighting.

Matibenga's activism continued in 1981 when she joined a trade union and represented workers working in shops, and challenged the oppression of African workers. She later joined the ZCTU, becoming its Vice President in 2003. She was elected in absentee in Geneva to be a governing member of the International Labour Organisation.

Lucia challenges the exclusion of women in central governing bodies, and believes that Women's Leagues, which perform as auxiliary bodies, oppress women because most of their members have been in the League since they were formed. She wants the women's organizations to become factories of leadership for women to be incorporated into main stream organizations. In MDC mainstream body there were only two women in 2011. Women in leadership should also serve as role models to encourage other women to join. She was impressed by women in Sudan Parliament who discuss real issues such as managing diversity in Africa.

**Matienga Margaret (MDC – T MP for Sunningdale 2011)**

**Margaret** was born in Harare in 1956 and grew up in Mbare. In 1974 she tried to cross into Mozambique to join the liberation struggle but was captured at the border and served three months in Chikurubhi Prison. She operated in Musana as a collaborator, travelling with freedom fighters carrying their weapons and cooking food until independence when she went into Assembly Points. She later joined the National Union of Clothing Industries Trade Union. She was instrumental in the formation of MDC. She became a ward councilor for Mbare but later resigned in solidarity with the suspension of Mayor Mudzuri.

Margaret experienced in-fighting within the party, especially from women. She also felt let down by WIPSU when she requested money for fuel during her campaign, but got help from Women's Trust and other well-wishers. As an MP she feels that female MPs from both parties are united, but it is difficult to make individual decisions because of party whipping system. Margaret wants more women into politics because they are focused and less corrupt than men. "If a man wants to fight a woman he uses another woman and it's very strong because if a woman fights you, she fights you…"she says, and encourages women to be strong, work together and support each other.

**Misihairabwi-Mushonga Priscilla (MDC - Minister of Regional Integration and International Cooperation 2011).**

**Priscilla** is a champion for women's rights, and was the only female negotiator in the GPA. She was elected MP for Glen Norah in 2000, after an election marred by political violence, and she believes that women should never have to be exposed to any violence of some sort.

"Unfortunately the people that bore the brunt of that violence were women… either in actually being physically beaten but because women have problem reporting even to the status quo, or being able to expose themselves to the media their stories went unreported. The same thing with cases of rape we know that a lot of sexual abuse reigning and we know how it is with sexual abuse and women coming out and saying you know I've been sexually abused. Not many women can actually do that"

Priscilla was appointed Minister of Regional Integration and International Cooperation, in the government of national unity, in the 2009. She was the MDC party Secretary General and MDC chief representative at JOMIC (Joint Monitoring and Implementation Committee) and COPAC the Constitutional Parliamentary Committee a committee in charge of writing the Zimbabwean constitution. Misihayirambwi Mushonga is Ambassador for Zimbabwe to the Kingdom of Sweden.

## Mlothswa Sthembile (MDC – T - was Senator fo Matobo). - 2011

The Late **Sithembile Mlothswa** (nee Sibanda) started politics when she was very young in Matopos. She joined the MDC and rose through the ranks, to the National Executive. The party asked her to become an MP for Matobo in 2008, and she won because she connected well with people from all wards. *"I don't regret to be a woman, I don't like to compete like a man, no, I want to be myself and yes, my contribution should be taken as a contribution from a person and not as a woman,"* she said.

She believed that the benefits of being a female in Parliament are the same as those of a man; because to be a leader of people one has to understand them. There are more women than men in the country, and men do not understand what women want, and only guess what women need because they are not women.

*"When women complain of something like maternity leave you feel it as a woman because you are part of it. As a woman you want to make policies which will help alleviate the problems faced by women and yourself because you know how it feels."*

## Mohadi Tambudzai (ZANU PF - Senator for Beitbridge - 2011)

**Tambudzai Mohadi** was born to a family of politics. Her father, Mleya, was arrested and imprisoned for life at Chikurubi as a D class prisoner. Her husband also went to war in 1972 and came back in 1980. Tambudzai became a Senator 2005, although she says she did not want to be a Senator because her husband was already an MP in the area, and did not want it to look like a family thing.

Mohadi practices what she preaches, and has groomed a number of women into politics in her area. She believes that most women fail to understand politics because they do not have idols to look up to. Women in Beitbridge, the border town of Zimbabwe and South Africa, are grateful to have Mama Mohadi as she is affectionately known in her area. Her political career is deeply rooted in her community.

At community level she has been involved in a number of projects while she was working for Agritex and then Lutheran. It is through this community work that her constituency asked her to stand and represent them. She encourages women to engage in self-help projects, more so if they are in politics, and believes that women are still oppressed by society; and that it will be very difficult to achieve 50/50 representation since at the moment they do not even have 30% representation.

## Mpariwa Paurina (MDC – T – Minister of Labour and Social Welfare, MP for Mufakose 2011)

A former OK Bazaars employee, Pauline's political activism started through trade unions, first representing OK workers in the Commercial workers Union until she joined the ZCTU. She became the first woman to be elected Chairperson of the Women's Council (ZCTU) in 1999. She was one of the founding members of the MDC. Paurina was the party's secretary for Labour, and she has the women, most who are involved in the vibrant informal sector, and youths, at her heart. She is concerned about the high levels of unemployment.

Mpariwa is constantly liaising with the ZCTU on the welfare of these women and youth. She looks to a future where the economic stability and integrity of Zimbabwe is restored and there is a more equitable distribution of resources.

In October 2003, Pauline was elected to the Pan African Parliament, and is still is a member.

## Mtingwende Tariro (ZANU PF – Senator for Gokwe North -2011)

**Tariro Mtingwende** was born in Nembudziya, Gokwe North, in 1959. She joined politics after 1980, and became the District Chair Person for Gokwe North (ZANU PF). She had a passion for women issues, and

wanted to make changes to their lives. She believed that it is important for women to join politics and participate in decision making because they are familiar with issues affecting them; including political violence and rape, while men can easily sneak away when things get tough.

Campaigning in the primaries was not easy for her. She lost to a man because she did not have enough resources. However, with the support of her District, she later campaigned to be a Senator and won. She believed that she was successful in her election because she worked well with people, especially women, because she had initiated many projects for women and youths.

Mtingende believed that it is important for women to be in Parliament because most constituencies represented by women tend to do better than those represented by men. Tariro was happy that her husband gave her supports, unlike most women who may want to advance in politics but their husbands hold them back especially when they feel threatened.

## Muchena Olivia (ZANU PF – Minster of Women's Affairs 2011)

**Olivia Muchena** was born in Mtoko in 1946 to politically conscious parents. She was a cabinet member, and Minister of Women's Affairs. Her father would sacrifice buying his children a loaf of bread to buy a newspaper so as to keep track of political issues and current affairs.

To her, politics is not only interesting and challenging, but keeps her mind, body and soul busy. She believes that having more women in parliament will help to address gender imbalances. Although women maybe interested in politics, their participation is limited by   social, cultural and economic factors. She believes 50/50 representation will be achieved through constitutional, legislative and educational measures.

Olivia has a PhD in Agriculture Extension Education from Iowa State University

## Muchenje Virginia (ZANU PF - Senator for Zvimba) - 2011

The late **Virginia Muchenje** started participating in politics in the mid 70s. She became awakened to gender activism since many parents during that time preferred to send the male-child to school, and the government had laws that oppressed women. Women were not allowed to apply for ID cards, or to vote. When she opened a Bank Account she had to ask her brother who was four years younger than her, to open the account. Women were also not allowed to apply for maternity leave. Women were also getting half salaries. As a temporary teacher she was getting paid £3.10 while a fellow male teacher was paid £7. During the war she supported the freedom fighters by giving them food, shelter and medicines.

After independence she became an active member of Zanu, working at grassroots level. She trained at Silveira House and Domboshava Training in Home Economics and Community Development in Rural Areas. She used the knowledge to work with women's projects to upgrade their lives. She wanted maternity leave to increase to between 4 and 6 months with full pay because child bearing is a national duty. Virginia encouraged women to pursue education because it creates opportunities to challenge oppression.

The number of female Councilors and Ministers will subsequently increase. Female councilors are more likely to focus on boreholes, clean water, clinics (welfare issues). In terms of campaigning, men tend to out-compete women because they have resources. They can also travel far and wide while the women are constrained by household commitments. These obstacles can be overcome if women are empowered financially through projects, and also through training in leadership skills. Women should also have access to loan.

**Muchihwa – Dandajena Rorana (MDC – T - Senator with 11 constituencies and 26 wards - 2011)**

**Rorana Dandajena's** political activism dates back to 1966, and during the liberation war she worked with the freedom fighters as a collaborator, carrying their

weapons and goods when they moved about in the country. However, she decided to join the MDC after the launch because of dissatisfaction with the government. She was the Chairperson for Resident Association (CRA). She faced political violence and was attacked and humiliated by female opponents. Rorana believes women can be each other's enemy, and pull each other down a lot.

In her political struggle she experienced more violence from women than men; although she also admits that she gained support from women's organizations like Wipsu. She believes that women need to be educated to respect and love themselves. "50/50 cannot be achieved if women don't respect and love each other".

**Muchinguri Oppah (Secretary of the Women's League in Zanu PF; Politburo member, and war veteran - 2011).**

**Oppah Muchinguri** was born in 1958, and joined the liberation war and received military training in guerilla warfare in Mozambique. She prides in the role played by women during the liberation war "I am a politburo member, but I'm also a war veteran who fought side by side with men…Women's emancipation did not just come without a price. We went through the war of liberation where we lost sons and daughters of Zimbabwe…It was not the easiest thing for us women in Zimbabwe…" she said, at a 50/50 representation workshop held in Harare on 3 August 2011.

She believes that women participation in decision making is the key to women's development. *"We have witnessed countries like South Africa performing so well to ensure that there are more women in decision-making. Same for Mozambique, and other countries…we have now decided as women of Zimbabwe that we need to speak with one voice,"* She continued.

Oppah feels that although Zimbabwe has almost 19 pieces of legislation in favour of women, more needs to be done in terms of implementation, including allocation of land to women, where 16% only of the land has been distributed to women. Muchinguri believes that economic empowerment for women will only be achieved if women stand up and fight for a gender balance; including *"increased participation in the educational system, political decision making workforce, and the more women become economically independent the less they are likely to remain living in difficult situations in their families, discriminatory workplaces and in unhappy marriages."*

Oppah held many portfolios after independence. She was the Private Secretary to the President from 1980-81; Deputy Minister of State for External Affairs from 1989-93; and Minister of Women's Affairs, Gender and Community Development from 2005 to 2009 among other portfolios.

Oppah Muchinguri Kashiri is Minister of Defence and War Veterans Affairs of Zimbabwe since 2018.

## Mujuru Joice (ZANU – PF - Vice President of Zimbabwe, MP Mount Darwin West - 2011)

**Joice Mujuru** was born Runaida Mugari in 1955 in Mt Darwin, and left Zimbabwe (then Rhodesia) for military training in 1973. She returned to Zimbabwe briefly in 1974 (battlefront). Joice assumed the name *Teurai Ropa* during the war, which became Teurai Ropa Nhongo after she married the late Solomon Mujuru (Rex Nhongo). In Mozambique she became a military trainer, and was the only female combatant to be an army commander.

She was Zimbabwe's first and youngest woman to have served as a Cabinet Minister in 1980 when she was appointed Minister of Youth, Education and Culture. She has since then held several ministerial posts. VP Mujuru believes all women should work for leadership roles and be accepted by men as leaders.

As a young woman Joice did not believe that boys were stronger than girls. *"She did not believe in the boy child being stronger or better than the girl child. Her belief was that we are all the same in the eyes of God. She is a real leader that one,"* said Shepherd, VP Mujuru's brother. Her mother Ambuya Mugari also said that although Joice was assertive as a young child, *"Obedience was her trademark and remains so to this day."*

VP Mujuru commands respect from people around her. She is humble, and a torch-bearer not only for Zimbabwean people, but for women especially and the Korekore people. *"I saw Teurai grow into the woman she is. Ndakaona humhandara hwake. Nhasi ndinefara kuti ndezveduwo kumaKorekore tava naVP,"* said Chief Kandeya. *"She is like a queen to us. We consider her to be just like a queen."* Zanu PF Provincial Chairman (Mashonaland West) Mr Edion Chiripanyanga said of VP Mujuru, *"I worked with her soon after independence and I must say I do not want to hear the gender balance argument. We do not approve of her nomination as a woman but because she is an able and deserving leader. She is a friendly yet stern woman and in her we have chosen as able a leader as President Mugabe himself."*

Joice Mujuru was fired from the post of Vice President by President Mugabe in 2015.

## Mutsvangwa Monica (ZANU – PF – MP Chimanimani - 2011)

**Monica Mutsvangwa** has been in politics since the age of 15 when she left the country to join the liberation struggle. Mutsvangwa would like to take a rather different approach to the usual and would like women to also involve men by educating them as they need to be enlightened. "But it's all about educating men, if you leave them out thinking that they know, how do they know? They have been brought up by us and we also, because of the cultural society that says this is for men and this for women, we just have to educate them."

Some of her responsibilities in parliament are as follows; she was part of the 25 select Committee Members who were spearheading COPAC, and she was the co-Vice Chair. She was the Chairperson of the portfolio committee on indigenization and empowerment which entails a lot of work. A delegate of the SADC Parliamentary forum and there she was Treasurer for the Executive for 2 years. She is also a technical advisor when it comes to reading bills to members of her party ZANU PF.

Mutsvangwa encourages women to be active in politics than to criticize from an aloof position. *"I feel we need to really get away from the idea of sitting back and reading and watching news and going on internet and then critisice. We need to do something as Zimbabweans and especially when we talk of women, we can never attain the 50/50 if women do not get out of that home and say look I need to participate in politics, we need women to get out there, it is so sad for a country which has had so many good policies about education to install few highly educated women in Parliament.*

**Ncube Spiwe (MDC-T Senator for Emganwini - 2011).**

**Spiwe Ncube** started political activism through trade unionism, and was one of the founding members of the MDC. She was elected as the Vice Organizing Secretary at the launch of MDC, and is in the MDC National Executive Committee. Spiwe acknowledges that being in politics has helped her to rise as a woman. *"Working as a politician is not easy but one has to be brave, one has to be sure of themselves, believing in yourself is very important if one has to be in politics and you should know what you want. You should not worry about what other people say about you ..."* she says. Spiwe says her husband is very supportive.

She feels that women are now fighting each other, instead of supporting each other. She would like to be given another term in Parliament to see her current projects reap fruits. *"We have done (projects) that we still want to see to the end if we could get the chance to go on we could achieve our goals. If we can have two terms but what is important is that as women we should support each other,"* Spiwe says.

She acknowledges that some of the challenges that she faces comes from her own party. *"...fighting each other is very retrogressive in a Party...if we don't achieve 50/50 across the board then it will not be achieved in politics. We might end up fighting for political positions as women and yet there is so much to do and there are other areas where we can go and be leaders, these areas can be feeders for politics."*

**Anastancia Ndhlovu (ZANU PF - MP for Shurugwi - 2011).**

**Anastancia** was the youngest MP for Zanu Pf in 2011. She was born on 6 October, 1980 in Shurugwi, and attended Charles Wraith Primary School in Shurugwi and Thornhill High School. She has a BSc Honours in Human Resources Management from the Midlands State University, and was then (2011) studying for an MSc in Human Resources Management. Anastancia was the National Deputy Secretary for Administration in the ZANU PF Youth League. She was the First Vice President – World Federation of Democratic Youth (WFDY). She is also a Human Resources Specialist – ZIMRA. She was elected Member of Parliament during the 2008 elections.

Anastancia hailed the Constituency Development Fund, but believes that rural areas should be awarded more money because they are large and have diverse needs different from urban areas. She used hers on a number of projects, including community empowerment projects targeting women. *"The projects changed many people's livelihoods especially in the area of education and health care,"* she said.

**Ndlovhu Patricia (ZANU PF - Councilor for Beitbridge - 2011)**

*Everything that we do is politics, even if we may choose not to believe it. Wherever you walk its politics! The water that you drink is politics!"* Said Patricia Ndlovu, who was the only woman councilor in Beitbridge in 2011, who feels it is important for women to be in politics as councilors and parliamentarians. She would like to encourage men to support their wives to be in politics, as women politicians are working towards 50/50 representation in parliament. She advises men not to be scared that women want to be in the highest decision making body in the country – politics. Councilor Ndlovu is part of the team that brought development to Beitbridge, a border post town which borders Zimbabwe and South Africa.

*"We encourage fathers (our husbands) to give us support we cannot be alone in this we need men to also support us. We have been advocating for women's representation in parliament as a lone voice. Isn't it nice to be called the husband of the President or Minister? My husband is happy to be the husband of a Councilor because he gets to know what is happening in our town/city. It is something to be proud about to know that your wife is one of the people bringing development to the city, which can only happen when a women is into active politics."* She is happy that her husband supports and encourages her, he even accompanies her to workshops and conferences to do with her work.

The councilor feels that at ward level there should be more women councilors and this will open the room for more female mayors; because mayors are voted by councilors and male councilors are likely to vote for male mayors.

**Nyamupinga Beater Beatrice (ZANU PF - Chairwoman Women's Parliamentarian Caucus – Goromonzi MP - 2011)**

**Beater** thinks that through Wipsu workshops many women are becoming more confident even to speak in front of intellectuals. She wanted 50/50 representation to be achieved by 2015, and to start in Parliament because *"that's where policies are made, and that's where favourable policies for women can be enacted".* Currently (in 2011) there were only 33 women out of 210 in the House of Assembly (representing on 1% out of 52% of the population into leadership).

*"We remain poor and when we are poor, elections have been commercialized, we will lose them but if we are economically empowered we will achieve because it is*

easy when you have resources", she says. Biata believes that because women are marginalized and outnumbered in Parliament, it is easy for male MPs to reject any constitutional proposal which favour women, hence 105 seats should be reserved for women.

## Nyoni Stembiso (ZANU PF – Minister of Medium and Small Scale Enterprises, MP Nkayi North - 2011)

"*Politics is a game that our mothers never taught us, our mothers taught us to care, to share and to serve. In fact my own mother, what I really got from her are those 3 values, so when you get into politics you find that there is so much that is strange to you, where positions sometimes matter more than loving, caring and serving each other. So as a woman you have to adjust, you have to create your space and say within this space*

*I will use these values that my mother taught me to get into power, if you don't do that you lose your womanhood, you lose your values and then you don't make the impact into politics and therefore I would have missed something in leadership if I hadn't come into politics. Politics has taught me to be my own woman regardless of what I have gone through, I have lost elections, I have won elections but all I have done is I have been myself in whatever I have done,*" said Sithembiso Nyoni, a woman who has been in politics for almost 30 years and is interested in development, her slogan is '*Zenzele*', a Ndebele word for do it for yourself, as development can never be given and cannot be imposed on the people, it has to be a force from inside that is watered and guided and assisted to grow.

Her speeches are about issues, about development and this has become her brand. Hon Nyoni believes that you can be a politician and still maintain your integrity.

Sthembiso Nyoni believes that through unity, women can achieve 50/50 representation in parliament. "*Rwanda has done it, Rwanda has surpassed this so yes it is possible*", she says.

## Sandi-Moyo Eunice Nomthandazo (ZANU PF - Politburo Member) - 2011

*It's good for women to venture into politics because politics decides the way a country should go, so women must be a part of that decision-making process but unfortunately sometimes personal egos hamper this set-up. We sometimes become too greedy, sometimes we want to challenge each other over nothing. I believe we should focus with the agenda of promoting women in the manner that it should be, the manner is don't challenge a woman who is already in a position, get the positions that the men are holding so that you become more in the set-up. What is the point of having 10 women out of 160 men, it does not work, then you go there and you fight for those 10 posts.* Words of advice come from a veteran politician **Eunice Sandi** whose political career spans 6 decades.

While the women's wing is good for development, she encourages women that it should not keep them away from the male domain especially during elections. You are there, you are fixed up, at a corner somewhere doing your own thing as women, that's why we are still challenging each other so much and because of that we are not getting there.

Sandi was born in Zimbabwe in 1946 but grew up in South Africa where she trained as a teacher. Her father was working as a police and that is where her mother came from, She returned to teach in Zimbabwe in 1960, and joined ZAPU. She was also involved in the Trade Union movement. She went to Zambia in 1975 where she trained as a soldier, and was sent to Germany to train in reconnaissance. She was a broadcaster for ZAPU.

She is the founder of an NGO Women in Business in the 1980'. She worked in Nkomo's office after independence, and was a politburo member for Zanu PF, and the Deputy Secretary for Women's League. She became Senator for Plumtree from 2006-2008.

## Shirichena Elina (ZANU PF - MP for Mberengwa South - 2011)

**Elina Shirichena** started politics around 1975. She worked for 10 years under the Ministry of Women's Affairs in Community development, before she became a provincial chairwoman, councilor and MP. Women chose her to represent them because she used to work with them doing some empowering projects. Her husband did not want her to join politics because he thought it was just good for single women, but the community leaders convinced him. Shirichena was groomed by Wipsu to become confident and develop leadership skills.

She works with 65 young women that she groomed who help her to run the constituency even in her absence. She empowered the young women financially through self-help projects so that they become confident. She believes that to achieve 50/50 women should join political parties of their choice and rise through the structures, and those women need to be united to implement projects and laws which benefit them.

Shirichena was appointed in the new ZANU PF Politburo in 2022 as Deputy Secretary for Disabilities.

## Sibanda – Mloyi Agnes (MDC-T - Senator for Gwabalanda - 2011)

Agnes Mloyi (nee Sibanda) was born in Godlwayo, but grew up in Kezi (same place with Joshua Nkomo) at a place called Dombodombo. She was a Zapu activist and rose through the structures of the party till she became District Chairperson for ZAPU. However, she later joined the MDC at its inception, becoming the first Interim District Chair for Women (Luveve), and later the Provincial Chairwoman (Women's Assembly). *"When there was a split in the MDC in 2005, it was us the women who made sure that the party did not die. When we had a congress I was elevated to the Main, so I was the one leading the Main Province in Bulawayo."*

She became a Senator in 2008. She believes that in politics one has to be brave, and that men don't think a woman can lead. She was the only woman who was leading a Province. She also believes that if there are more women in parliament they can pass bills that are favourable to women, and deny those that oppress women. However, she thinks the main problem with women is that most of them are not educated, while the educated ones do not want to be involved in politics. "We have been asking educated women to join us than to criticize us by saying uneducated people don't know anything and yet the educated don't want to join politics; the bottom line is that we do not support each other," she says.

## Sibanda Dorcas (MDC T - MP for Bulawayo Central and Parliament's Deputy Chief Whip - 2011)

45 year-old **Dorcas Sibanda** (in 2011) now she is 57, was born in Tshabalala, Bulawayo. She joined ZAPU during the colonial era, and the MDC in 1999 through a Trade Union, Zimbabwe Association of Railway

Union (ZARU). She rose through the ranks, and was elected MP for Bulawayo Central in 2008, and also a Deputy Chief Whip in Parliament. Confident to move motions and participate in debates, Dorcas acknowledges that at times resentment comes from fellow women parliamentarians.

She is a mother to four daughters aged between twenty and thirty-eight. Politics runs in her family. Her father, Gowe Sibanda, was an active ZAPU member, while her three brothers were ZIPRA fighters.

She believes empowering a woman is empowering a whole nation.

## Stevenson Trudy (former MDC MP for Harare North – 2011)

The late **Gertrude Stevenson** was born in the USA in 1944, and describes herself as a war-baby. Her father was a northerner while her mother was a southerner, and there was antagonism between people of the

north with people of the south then. She was therefore enlightened to political consciousness and human rights at an early age. Her mother was not fully accepted by her father's family.

She was the MDC MP for Harare North Constituency from 2000 to 2008, and was a member of the National Education Advisory Board. A human and women's rights activist, she founded a number of organizations. She was Zimbabwean Ambassador to Senegal and the Gambia. Trudy passed on in August 2018.

Gertrude moved to England with her mother where she later graduated with a degree at the University of Reading. With her husband Stewart Stevenson, the couple travelled to Uganda in 1969 and left in 1972, and went to settle in Swaziland where Stevenson taught at a primary school. From 1976-78 they were in Zambia, and after a short period living in Rome, they came to Zimbabwe in 1980 shortly after the nation celebrated its independence. Stevenson taught French and Italian at an elite private girl's school, Arundel Secondary School. Her life changed dramatically in 1988 when her husband left her.

*"This is when I understood women's problems, as my husband left me poor and I had to look after three children," she said. "It was difficult to serve him with divorce notices as we did not know where he was until we found him in 1992, and the divorce went through."*

Stevenson loved her adopted nation and acquired Zimbabwean citizenship in 1989, and plunged into women's and civic politics issues.

## Zinyemba Margaret (ZANU PF - MP for Chiweshe 2011)

The late **Margaret Zinyemba** was born February 1939, and as a girl child her parents sent her younger brother to school (patriarchy) before her, and this helped to shape her activism as she sought to challenge gender imbalances and racism. She served Mazowe Rural District Council for 16 years as a Councillor. She was chosen by a delegation of men in her area to become an MP. Her constituency was reserved for women, so she stood against three women at primaries. Margaret acknowledged that the current political field poses challenges to women who want to engage in politics, because people nominate themselves, and there is also bribery and corruption (vote buying).

There is now too much competition, which threatens

women's unity. Women also lack resources (financial) to launch successful campaigns against men. However, she believed that it is important to have more women MPs because women are naturally nation builders, and in transparency and honest. She told people in her constituency the truth about what she can achieve and what she could not.

Through the Constituency Development Fund Margaret assisted schools and clinics in her constituency with resources. She also bought sports kits for children in schools to encourage physical fitness through sport, and helped some people to access loans for agriculture. She wanted to develop roads (infrastructure) in her area to make some places accessible. She was also helping women to form clubs, as well as helping people in her constituency to apply for prospecting mining licenses. She wanted more women to engage in politics and wanted more female parliamentarians as this is the only way that women can challenge oppression and improve their welfare.

A message for women is that they should not let poverty decided their fate, because men can exploit that to their advantage.

Margaret Zinyemba passed on in 2015.

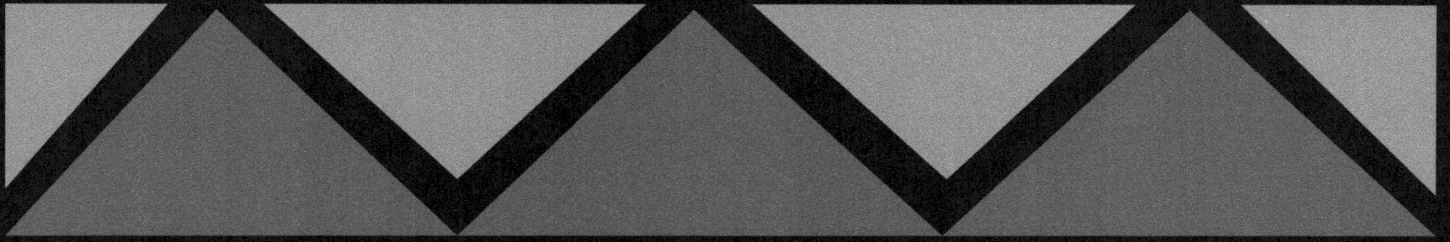

# PHOTO
# CREDITS

# PHOTO CREDITS FOR THE MAIN STORY

| | |
|---|---|
| Mbuya Nehanda | Bulawayo24.com |
| Queen Lozkey | National Archives of Zimbabwe |
| Women Building a home | National Archives of Zimbabwe |
| Woman telling stories | PIndula.org |
| Modjadji | National Archives of Zimbabwe |
| Monomotapa Kingdom | facebook.com |
| Ambuya Nehanda | National Archives of Zimbabwe |
| Pioneer Column | National Archives of Zimbabwe |
| Women in the liberation struggle | Zenzo Nkobi |
| Virginia Sillah | Youtube.com |
| Bebe Mellows | Youtube.com |
| Mbuya Nehanda | The Herald Zimbabwe |
| Mbuya Nehanda signpost | sage publications |
| Mbuya Nehanda Maternity Hospital | The Herald Zimbabwe |
| Queen Lozikeyi | National Archives of Zimbabwe |
| Queen Lozikeyi | National Archives of Zimbabwe |
| Queen Lozikeyi | Newsday Zimbabwe |
| Queen Lozikeyi sitting with the other royal wives | Amakhosikazi media |
| Tawse Jolly | Wikipedia .com |
| Tawse Jolly sitting in the 1923 Rhodesian government | www.rhodesia.me.uk |
| KM Davidson | www.rhodesia.me.uk |
| KM Davidson in the 1929 Government | www.rhosedia.me.uk |
| Muriel Rosin | Muriel Rosin |
| Muriel Rosin in the Federal Government – | National Archives of Zimbabwe |
| Ruth Chinamano | Biddy Patridge |
| Joushua Nkomo, Joseph Msika, Josiah Chinamano | |
| Chinamano and Ruth Chinamano at Gonakudzingwa | Bester Kanyama |
| Ruth Chinamano | Diana Mitchell |

# PHOTO CREDITS FOR THE MAIN STORY

| | |
|---|---|
| Ruth Chinamano talking to Eillen Haddon | Eileen Haddon |
| Muriel Rosin Book-The Visionary Muriel E. Rosin MBE, 1909- 1999 by R | David Rosin |
| Muriel Rosin | Joyce Jenje Makwenda Collection Archives |
| Joana Mafuyana | Bulawayo24.com |
| Joana Mafuyana and family | Bulawayo24.c0m |
| Sally Mugabe | Ghanaweb |
| Sally Mugabe and Robert Mugabe | Blackpast |
| Maria Msika | The Herald Zimbabwe |
| Maria and Joseph Msika | The Herald Zimbabwe |
| Maud Muzenda | The Herald Zimbabwe |
| Sunny Takawira | Gertrude Takawira |
| Sunny Takawira and family | Gertrude Takawira |
| Julia Zvobgo | Veritas Women |
| Eddisson Zvobgo | Wikipedia.com |
| Victoria Chitepo | IMS Vintage Photos |
| Victora and Herbert Chitepo | The Sunday Mail Zimbabwe |
| Stella Madzimbamuto | The Sunday News Zimbabwe |
| Stela and Daniel Madzimbamuto | Wikipedia .com |
| Betty Mtero | Fidelis Zvomuya |
| Helen Mangwende | National Archives of Zimbabwe |
| Tsitis Munyati | Nigel Munyati |
| Mrs Lesabe | Joyce Jenje Makwenda Collection Archive |
| Mrs Mutsvairo | Joyce Jenje Makwenda Collection Archive |
| Angeline Masuku | The Herald Zimbabwe |
| Stembiso Nyoni | Fidelis Zvomuya |
| Elina Shirichena | Fidelis Zvomuya |
| Jenia Manyeruke | Fidelis Zvomuya |
| Gladys Mabhiza | Fidelis Zvumya |

# PHOTO CREDITS FOR THE MAIN STORY

| | |
|---|---|
| Mavis Chidzonga | The Herald Zimbabwe |
| Margaret Dongo | Joyce Jenje Makwenda Collection Archive |
| Canaan Jenje | Joyce Jenje Makwenda Collection Archive |
| Eileen Haddon | Eileen Haddon |
| Mike Haddon | Joyce Jenje Makwenda Collection Archives |
| City Quads | Joyce Jenje Makwenda Collection Archive |
| De Black Evening Follies | Joyce Jenje Makwenda Collection Archive |
| Thenjiwe Lesabe | Newsday Zimbabwe |
| Emmanuel Jenje | Joyce Jenje Makwenda Collection Archives |
| Diana Mitchell | Hoover Institution |
| Centre Party Logo | Wikipedia.com |
| Diana Mitchell with John Indi | Diana Mitchell |
| Diana Mitchell | Diana Mitchell |
| Jane Ngwenya | Ruth Weiss, 1986 |
| Eunice Sandi Moyo | Newsday Zimbabwe |
| Joyce Mujuru and Victoria Chitepo | Fidelis Zvomuya |
| Naomi Nhiwatiwa | National Archives of Zimbabwe |
| Joyce Mujuru | The Herald Zimbabwe |
| Joyce Mujuru | The Herald Zimbabwe |
| Margaret Dongo | Margaret Dongo |
| Esther Mhembere | National Archives of Zimbabwe |
| Vester Saungweme | National Archives of Zimbabwe |
| Poshi Mugudubi | National Archives of Zimbabwe |
| Joyce Xahe | National Archives of Zimbabwe |
| Joyce Chenzira Mutasa | National Archives of Zimbabwe |
| Vishet Dziruni | National Archives of Zimbabwe |

# PHOTO CREDITS FOR THE MAIN STORY

| | |
|---|---|
| Ruth Chinamano | Joyce Jenje Makwenda Collection Archives |
| Betty Mtero and Victoria Chitepo | Fidelis Zvomuya |
| Mavis Chidzonga | The Herald Zimbabwe |
| Prsicilla Misihairabwi Mushonga | The Herald Zimbabwe |
| Thokozani Khupe | The Sunday News Zimbabwe |
| Monica Mutsvangwa | Gambakwe media |
| Women in Parliament | open parliament Zimbabwe |
| Tatenda Mavetera | spikedmedia.co.zw |
| Fadzai Mahere | EJS Centre |
| Sandra Ndebele | Gambakwe media |
| Elisabeth Valerio | Pindula News |
| Eunice Sandi Moyo | Pindula news |
| Angeline Makuvarara | National Archives of Zimbabwe |
| Amina Hughes | The Herald Zimbabwe |
| Trudy Stevenson | The Herald Zimbabwe |
| Jaqueline Zwambila | The Herald Zimbabwe |
| Gertrude Takawira | Gertrude Takawira |
| Thandiwe Dumbutchena | Facebook.com |
| Rudo Chitiga | Rudo Chitiga |

# PHOTO CREDITS FOR SHORT STORIES - WOMEN POLITICIANS/ PARLIAMENTARIANS

| NAME | PHOTOGRAPHER |
| --- | --- |
| Bhudha Masara Sibusisiwe | Fidelis Zvomuya |
| Bhuka Flora | Fidelis Zvomuya |
| Chabuka Keresenzia | Fidelis Zvomuya |
| Chaderopa Fungai | Fidelis Zvomuya |
| Chikava Betty | Fidelis Zvomuya |
| Chimbudzi Alice | Fidelis Zvomuya |
| Chinomona Mabel | Fidelis Zvomuya |
| Dete Agnes | Fidelis Zvomuya |
| Dongo Margaret | Margaret Dongo |
| Dube-Gombami Gladys | Fidelis Zvomuya |
| Goto Rosemary | Fidelis Zvomuya |
| Holland Sekai | Jeff Milanzi |
| Karenyi Lynette | Fidelis Zvomuya |
| Katsande Aqilina | Fidelis Zvomuya |
| Katyamaenza Viriginia | Fidelis Zvomuya |
| Khumalo Tabitha | Fidelis Zvomuya |
| Khupe Thokozane | Fidelis Zvomuya |
| Mabhiza Gladys | Fidelis Zvomuya |
| Madzongwe Edna | Jeff Milanzi |
| Mahofa Shuvai | Fidelis Zvomuya |
| Mahoka Sarah | Fidelis Zvomuya |
| Majome Fungai Jessie | Jeff Milanzi |

# PHOTO CREDITS FOR SHORT STORIES - WOMEN POLITICIANS/ PARLIAMENTARIANS

| | |
|---|---|
| Makone Theresa | Fidelis Zvomuya |
| Mandaba Maina Imelda | Fidelis Zvomuya |
| Mangami Dorothy | Fidelis Zvomuya |
| Manyeruke Jenia | Fidelis Zvomuya |
| Maposhere Darcus | Fidelis Zvomuya |
| Masaiti Evelyn | Fidelis Zvomuya |
| Masuku Angeline | Wikipedia |
| Matamisa Editor | Fidelis Zvomuya |
| Matibenga Lucia | Fidelis Zvomuya |
| Matienga Margaret | Fidelis Zvomuya |
| Mathuthu Thokozile | Jeff Milanzi |
| Misihairabwi-Mushonga Priscilla | Newsday Zimbabwe |
| Mlothswa Sthembile | Fidelis Zvomuya |
| Mohadi Tambudzai | Fidelis Zvomuya |
| Mpariwa Paurina | Fidelis Zvomuya |
| Mtingwende Tariro | Fidelis Zvomuya |
| Muchena Olivia | Fidelis Zvomuya |
| Muchenje Virginia | Fidelis Zvomuya |
| Muchihwa-D Rorana | Fidelis Zvomuya |
| Muchinguri oppah | Newdsay.co.zw |
| Mudau Metrine | Fidelis Zvomuya |
| Mujuru Joice | The Herald.co.zw |

# PHOTO CREDITS FOR SHORT STORIES - WOMEN POLITICIANS/ PARLIAMENTARIANS

| | |
|---|---|
| Mutsvangwa Monica | The Herald.co.zw |
| Ncube Spiwe | Fidelis Zvomuya |
| Ndlovu Anastancia | Fidelis Zvomuya |
| Ndlovu Patricia | Fidelis Zvomuya |
| Nyamupinga B Beatrice | Fidelis Zvomuya |
| Nyoni Sthembiso | Fidelis Zvomuya |
| Sandi-Ndlovu Eunice | Fdelis Zvomuya |
| Shirichena Ellina | Fidelis Zvomuya |
| Sibanda-Mloyi Agnes | Fidelis Zvomuya |
| Sibanda Dorcas | Fidelis Zvomuya |
| Stevenson Trudy | The Herald.co.zw |
| Zinyemba Margaret | Fidelis Zvomura |

# ACKNOWLEDGEMENTS AND DEDICATION

My gratitude goes to all those who made this book possible, mainly Open Society Initiative for Southern Africa (OSISA) for funding the editing and printing of this book – History of Women Politicians of Zimbabwe. In addition I would like to thank the following people at OSISA – Special thanks to Lucinda Van Den Heever and Sipho Malunga for believing in this project and for seeing its importance, and also for their support and encouragement. Special mention goes to Alice Kwaramba Kanengoni for the encouragement and support. I would also like to thank the OSISA Team who assisted me in different ways. I will always be grateful to you all.

I am grateful to ZIMRIGHTS (Zimbabwe Human Rights Association) for facilitating the project – Dzikamai Bere, Tafadzwa Mutiti, Amos Madzinire and Tsitsi Tambura.

My appreciation to MISA for being there when I needed help, while working on the project. In particular Anne Musodza, Nyasha Nyakunu, Ophias Kimbini and Tabani Moyo. I would also like to make mention to ZIFF who were there to assist in various ways – Solomon Maramba and Nakai Matema.

The National Archives of Zimbabwe played an all –embracing role as an invaluable store house of historical material. Thank you.

I would like to thank all those who supported the project in various ways. I am very thankful to: My sister Ambassador Rudo Chitiga you believed in this project and you could see it where it is now. Hope Chigudu my sister, your frank views on women politicians have helped

# ACKNOWLEDGEMENTS AND DEDICATION

My appreciation also goes to the following: Jeff Milanzi always there on most of my projects including this one. Livingstone Muchefa, for your assistance in research. Nigel Munyati, Linnette Frewin and David Nelson for Mama Tsitsi Munyati's photos and stories. The Msika Family, in particular Inno Msika, Gari Msika and Max Msika for Mama and Baba Msika's photos. The late Fidelis Zvomuya for most of the photos. Pathisa Nyathi thank you so much for allowing us to tap from your well of wisdom. Alexio Murombo for the advice and support, and Vitalis Jeremiah for the support in so many ways.

I will always be grateful to Yolanda Birivadi my administrator who has worked tirelessly on many of my projects and in particular this one. She says this was one was the most challenging one - but we made it. We are here. Thank you.

I will always be indebted to my first teachers my parents.

I am very grateful to my parents Canaan Mateza Dube (my mother) and David Jenje (my father) for encouraging me in my initial stages of research in music and this gave birth to a lot of other researches including this one on the History of Women Politicians. I will forever be grateful for the stories that you told me which brought out the storyteller in me in different ways. Your understanding of local and international politics impacted on how I understand politics and my Pan African views. My understanding of politics was when the two of you would discuss about political figures and issues. Your stories about your families – how there were affected by politics - socially and economical made me want to understand more about our political history. This made me want to research on politics and in particular about women who are so underrepresented in the political structures of our country. You held my hand and you taught me and encouraged me that it was

# ACKNOWLEDGEMENTS AND DEDICATION

okay to dream. Ngiyabing Kakhulu, ndinotenda zvikuru.

My parents' parents *(uGogo loMkhulu – Ambuya naSekuru)* (My grandparents), thank you so much for the stories. Sekuru (Grandfather) Jenje Marko Mhembere and (Grandfather) *uKhulu uTarara Mateza Dube* you used to tell me stories to do with how great your tribes were. How they conqured other tribes. That was politics! It was as if the two of you were from the same mother and yet you were raised miles apart from each other. Khulu Mateza from Bulawayo and Sekuru Jenje from Harare but you spoke the same language that of being great tribes. Sekuru Jenje you used to tell me how great the VaShawasha were and Khulu Tarara you used to tell me how great the Ndebele Nation was, which came from the Zulu Nation. You were telling this small child called Joyce and she was struggling to conceive it at that young age but you did not stop and this was kept in a hard drive in my head and it helped create the politician in me. *Ngiyabonga Kakhulu, Ndinotenda zvikuru.*

Gogo Malandu Mangena Mateza Dube the stories you told me about how one has to look out for certain things in their stages of life saw me through life itself. Your community leadership Gogo Malandu, as a strong woman that you were, inspired me and taught me how strong you were as an African woman even if your digniy had been tempered with by the colonialists but you were this stong woman that I talk about and I will continue to talk about Malandu Mangena – Gogo wami (my Grandmother). Ambuya vangu VaChihute (my grandmother VaChihute) you were the only one who was not a story teller amomgst my six parents, although you later became one when all the five had left this world and I was left with you. You sort of wraped up what the other parents had told me and brought a bit of some clarity and now I could understand some of it because I was a bit older. You were not a story

# ACKNOWLEDGEMENTS AND DEDICATION

teller like the other five because you were very hurt about how you left Chishawasha and you later told me that you were the last to resist when your land was taken in Chishawasha. You had to walk from Chishawasha to Salisbury carrying my father David on the back. Your destination was just Salisbury with no address –a dark cold place!! You and other early urban settlers settled in this cold, dark place . All you wanted was how you could give your children, your grandchildren a good life and you worked so much, you broke your back to do the best that you can. With other women you became the founders of the informal sector and for you, economic power was important. It is what women politicians are discovering that without economic power they cannot go far. Thank you for paving the way.

My children, thank you so much you have been amazing in particular Sasani Naome. You have walked with me on this road as working on a project like this one has its downs and ups and you have been there all the way. Discussing the project while I was working on it and after, this has been such a wonderful experience to have the the love and good energies . Thank you so much aNyampande – muje kutali ndimotu. I would also like to thank my son Simbarashe whom I sometimes engange in discussions in politics of our Africa, Diaspora and Zimbabwe. His understanding of black politics has been amazing although sometimes in a very radical way, but inspiring. My grandchildren – Nontando Mya, Thamsanqa Emanuel, Jabulani Joshua and Thando. You make my world go round. Your energies are just amazing – You are the wind beneath my wings!!! Love and hugs!!!

My appreciation also goes to: my sisters in particular Juliet who has been with me throughout the project, the lows and highs, you were there. I can not not list what you have done for me throughout this

# ACKNOWLEDGEMENTS AND DEDICATION

journey. Amazing love sis. Gertrude Takawira my sister where do I start– the list is too long. You always preach love and you practice it. I would also like to thank my brothers - Emanuel if you were here you would have been proud of me. Alexio and amai Diva muroora thank you so much for everything. The good energies were amazing. Sekuru Farai for always being there in so many ways in almost all my projects. The love Sekuru is amazing, the caring, I can go on and on. Thank you so much my sisters and brothers for the support and encouragement always.

I would like to thank all those who have been there for me while working on this project - my family, children, grandchildren, sisters, brothers, relatives, collegues, friends, organisations, Institutions.

Last but not least we would to thank Hakeem Frank, Jonathan Gankila and Learnmore Chilumba for going an extra mile for this project. We really appreciate the support from Sable Press. Thank you so much.

Time and space do not permit the mention of several contributors, for their liberal assistance in the fulfilment of my aspired project book.

Thank you all!

# ABOUT
# THE
# AUTHOR

# Joyce Jenje Makwenda

**Joyce Jenje Makwenda** is an award winning Producer, Journalist, Artist and Ethnomusicologist. She is also an Independent Scholar, Archivist, Historian, Researcher, Author, and Lecturer. She has 38 years of working experience covering areas of early urban culture, music, politics, education, religion, media, fashion, sex and sexuality (taboo issues) and cultural issues and women's histories in Zimbabwe. Joyce Jenje Makwenda has written a number of books and novels. She has produced and directed award-winning film documentaries.

She established in Zimbabwe, one of the biggest private social history collection/archive at her house (her three-bedroom cottage), which consists of interviews on - early urban culture, music, politics, education, religion, media, fashion, sex and sexuality (taboo issues) and cultural issues and women's histories in Zimbabwe., on audio and video, and

# About the Author

most of the interviews are transcribed and also press cuttings, photos, LP's and music artefacts, such as gramophones, typewriters etc. for scholarly and historical purposes, and for posterity. A full research catalogue and a women's catalogue are housed in the Joyce Jenje Makwenda Collection Archive (JJMCA).

## HISTORY OF WOMEN POLITICIANS OF ZIMBABWE

Joyce Jenje Makwenda started researching on the History of Women Politicians of Zimbabwe in the early 1990's and has been writing articles in the newspapers, magazines and journals. Joyce has interviewed around 65 women and her research goes as far back as the pre-colonial era to today. The interviews are on print, audio and video.

Her work has seen her being awarded with accolades and some of them are:

### AWARDS
▸ Special Mention: Zimbabwe Township Music Documentary: Southern African Film Festival - (1993).
▸ Best T.V. Producer of the year (Entertainment, music, drama) - The National Journalists and Media Awards for 1993 - Zimbabwe, Sponsored by REUTERS.
▸ Second Best T.V. Producer of The Year 1994 National Journalistic and Media Awards Zimbabwe Sponsored by REUTERS (1994).
▸ Freelance Woman Journalist of the Year 1999 funded by UNIFEM hosted by The Federation of Media Women of Zimbabwe (1999)
▸ Population Development and Gender Writer of The Year (Overall Winner) funded by UNFPA hosted by Zimbabwe Union of Journalists (ZUJ) (2002)
▸ Special Award the Triple T Award - "Tackling Taboo Topics" (New Category) – Gender Links/GEMSA Awards - Gender Mainstreaming –– Johannesburg (2010)
▸ Special Mention: Women in the Arts Festival (WAFEST) for done in the arts – HARARE (2015).
▸ National Arts Merit Awards (NAMA) Legends 2021 Award - Awarded for Ethnomusicology and Archiving (the Joyce Jenje Makwenda Collection Archive – JJMCA).

www.ingramcontent.com/pod-product-compliance
Lightning Source LLC
Chambersburg PA
CBHW080135270326
41926CB00021B/4499